Lead Less, Build More

Create Systems That Scale Without You

Suresh MK

Lead Less, Build More

Copyright ©2026 by Suresh MK

All rights reserved. No part of this publication may be reproduced, distributed, or transmitted in any form or by any means, including photocopying, recording, or other electronic or mechanical methods, without the prior written permission of the author. For permission requests, please write an email to suresh@mksuresh.com

ISBN Paperback: 978-93-5635-560-6
ISBN Hardback: 978-93-5655-064-3

Published by:
Simplified Education Systems

Edition 1 Ver220126-1

To my mother,
my first spiritual guide —
who held me steady through every high and low,
and who now watches from above
with a tenderness that still shapes my days.
Your quiet strength has been my compass.

To my father,
my lifelong role model —
who taught me the art of balancing work with life,
effort with ease,
ambition with presence.
The very first chapter of this book exists because of you.

To my gurus,
Mahavatar Babaji and **Chandrasekharendra Saraswati (Maha Periyava)**,
whose grace, wisdom, and unseen guidance
have shaped my inner journey
far more than these pages can ever express.

This book is a small offering
to all the light you have poured into me.

To my wife,
who led in the quiet spaces. When life pulled me away,
you became the rhythm that held our home—
deciding, steadying, sustaining,
without titles, timelines, or applause.

You showed me that leadership
does not need a stage,
that presence can be felt even in absence,
and that what endures is often built softly.

Long before I wrote about
leading without being in the room,
I watched you live it.

This book carries that lesson—
and my gratitude—
between every line.

Foreword

Most management books offer hacks; Suresh MK offers a fundamental reset. Having worked closely with Suresh more than a decade ago during my tenure as EY's Global CFO, I saw first-hand his ability to navigate immense operational complexity with calm, systemic focus.

At that time, we were at a critical juncture: building the plan to globalize EY's finance functions. We were moving from a world where finance was owned and run country-by-country toward a unified, globalized model supported by a new ERP system. It was a massive undertaking that required moving away from "heroic" leadership—where individual leaders personally solved local crises through sheer force of will—toward a scalable, global architecture.

In these pages, Suresh deconstructs that "Hero's Trap". He challenges the dangerous pattern where leaders rescue their teams from recurring crises rather than fixing the underlying broken processes. He introduces a necessary new vocabulary for the modern executive: the "Directly Responsible Individual" (DRI), the "No List", and "AI as a Co-Leader".

At the heart of his philosophy is a powerful realization we lived during our transformation journey: trust is not a "soft" skill; it is infrastructure. By treating trust as the operating system and clarity as a mandatory requirement, Suresh shows us how to build "pods" that move with startup speed even within global giants.

Whether you are a middle manager or a CEO, Lead Less, Build More will give you the courage to let go and the tools to build something that truly scales. Suresh has captured the essence of what it takes to build an organization that can thrive without depending on any single person to save it.

Michael Ventling,
Retired Global CFO, EY

Practitioner Perspective

Leadership is often described as visibility, decisiveness, and speed. Over the years, I've also observed that leadership that lasts and leaders who make the most impact are usually quieter. This type of leadership spends less time intervening and more time setting things up for the future, so they don't need intervention in the first place. That is what struck me most as I read *Lead Less, Build More*.

I have known Suresh for many years — as a colleague, a fellow practitioner, and someone who has spent a long time inside large, complex systems trying to make them work better. Long before this book existed, I had seen the thinking behind it in action. We have travelled the world together for work and used the time discussing challenges at work and a variety of other things. Over the past couple of years, I have been repeatedly nudging Suresh to structure his experience and thoughts into the form of a book, so others can benefit from it. It was a brilliant experience to see how Suresh organized writing this book as a project and completed this with lots of sincerity. Suresh and I have shared several years of our professional journey at EY, and it is a pleasure reminiscing through several of the anecdotes that Suresh has very appropriately woven into the chapters of his book. I believe this book should offer readers a great insight into the variety of leadership challenges one can be expected to navigate while leading large global multi-cultural teams.

The long-term lens running through the book resonated strongly with me. Whether in technology, automation, or people development, sustainable value rarely comes from one big move. It comes from many small, consistent decisions, reinforced over time. Capability compounds. Culture compounds. Even good judgment compounds when it is allowed to spread beyond a single leader.

There is also restraint in this book, which I appreciate. It does not romanticize delegation, nor does it suggest that leadership is about stepping away entirely. Instead, it argues for presence at the right level — knowing when to guide, when to challenge, and when to let the system do its work.

The chapters that explore AI as a co-leader, ownership at scale, and new ways of organizing work reflect realities leaders are currently facing. Intelligence today is distributed. Decisions need to happen closer to the work. The role of leadership will increasingly be to create conditions where this can happen without losing coherence or control.

The book's epilogue adds a thoughtful pause. Leadership as permission rather than possession is not a metaphor that fades quickly. In professional life, roles change. Titles move on. What remains is what one helped built — and whether it continues to work when we are no longer in the middle of it.

Suresh has not framed this as a book of answers. It is a book of reflection. Suresh asks readers to look honestly at where they may be holding on too tightly, where systems could be doing more of the work, and where letting go might create more value. If this book causes you to intervene a little less, trust a little more, and invest patiently in systems that outlast you, it will have done its job. As Suresh has always told me, leadership that endures rarely announces itself.

Shailendra Saxena,
Partner, EY

Academic Perspective

Leadership debates and discussion in current times have started to increasingly recognize the fact that organizational scale is very rarely achieved through individual heroics; rather in most cases, the same is achieved through the systematic cultivation of structures, processes, and cultures that can function independent of any single individual / actor. To that end, Lead Less, Build More makes a very important timely and compelling contribution to this ongoing conversation. Drawing on extensive first hand as well as secondary cross-national experience in executive leadership and transformation, Suresh MK articulates a framework that advances a very distinct systems-oriented understanding of organizational growth.

The book challenges a persistent and long held view win corporate and entrepreneurial environments that the most capable and influential leaders are those who assume disproportionately high responsibility, make the most decisions directly or is involved in most decision making aspects when not involved directly, and remain perpetually as the epicentre of organizational activity. While this model may yield short-term gains, Suresh identifies its long-term limitations such as individual dependency, bottlenecks, and ultimately stagnation and decline in performance. The alternative that Suresh proposes is neither theoretical nor idealistic; rather, it is based on field-tested methodologies developed across large-scale financial and organizational transformations across various countries.

The uniqueness of this books is the way it suggests the shift from the rhetoric to the architecture, in the context of empowerment within an organization. The book outlines the different mechanisms for autonomy in decision making, system design, accountability structures, and cultural reinforcement – factors that enable teams to operate boldly and competently without continuous oversight and subject to micromanagement. In doing so, it redefines leadership not as the art of doing more, but as the art of enabling more to be done by others.

Lead Less, Build More is therefore simultaneously a critique of traditional leadership expectations as well as a blueprint for sustainable scale. It will serve practitioners, academics, and students alike who seek to understand how modern organizations can grow without exhausting their leaders, and how leadership efficacy must evolve in a world defined by complexity, interdependence, and rapid change.

Sankarshan Basu,
Professor (Finance and Accounting), IIM Bangalore

Reactions to
Lead Less, Build More

I met Suresh last year, when we went on a "Kailash Manasarovar yatra" together. We discovered that both of us have some common interests and this includes writing. I was impressed with his clarity of thoughts and yearning for learning all the time. This is reflected in his first book - *Lead less, Build more*. Suresh's axiom of leadership is based on a foundation of trust and empowerment and this resonated very well with me.

Suresh invited me to read his book even before it got published and offer him constructive feedback. This again reflects his maturity and reflective nature.

His book on leadership is a treat for practitioners, consultants and students as it is difficult to elucidate a complex subject like leadership in a very grounded and simple language. I loved all his examples from real life experiences, which all of us as readers will appreciate.

Wish you all the best Suresh for great success in this book and many more books to follow.

S Ramesh Shankar, Chief Joy Officer, Hrishti & Former CHRO, Siemens – South Asia

In a landscape saturated with fast moving business trends, this management masterpiece stands out as an essential compass for today's business leaders. It connects strategic theory with the realities of daily team dynamics. It provides actionable blueprint for fostering innovation while maintaining steady productivity.

The book's chapters offer real life examples of reputable companies with practical guidance on managing stress and delivering more by empowering your team. Whether you are an experienced executive or an aspiring leader, this guide challenges conventional hierarchies and encourages you to lead with both empathy and data-driven precision.

It is not just a book—it is a vital toolkit for the 2026 workplace.

Well done Suresh!

> ***Haren Bhat, Retired CFO and Senior Finance Executive***

As our world hurtles through mind-boggling changes, in every dimension, so many leaders feel the critical need to speed up, do more, regulate more, de-risk every move and plan themselves into oblivion! It takes a bold, inspired and courageous leader to hit the pause button and challenge all these and many more leadership myths. Suresh has penned wonderfully succinct, deeply human and practical, inspiring messages to all of us. Each insight and guidance will ease the massive stress we find ourselves under as we navigate the disruptions and stresses of our new multi-polar and almost incomprehensible world, where all the rules we know and trust seem to have evaporated!

Suresh writes simply yet profoundly, offering personal lessons learned, and reminding us that movement does not equate to momentum. He skillfully reminds us to breathe, to make time and pace to allow our human mental machinery to process complexity in its own natural way, and to trust our fellow colleagues, trust the process of thinking with clarity only gained by creating space for the puzzle pieces to fall into their natural and best fitting spaces.

This book will grip you with its simplicity yet deeply valuable and very practical insights and tools. Pay attention and your leadership will never look back! One of the valuable insights of this "hard to put down" book is that the basic elements of humanness that we all value in our families and closest friends are what make leaders valuable. This is significant in our new future where artificial intelligence, smart systems, robots and agentic processing will take over so much of what leaders needed to deliver in the past.

The good news is that by following the essential features of deeply centred humanness that Suresh so articulately discusses, leaders will become even more valuable and relevant!

This is a "Must read" and "must share" book.

Anton Musgrave, Futurist and Global Business Strategist

This is one if those books I could relate to in an instant. Pragmatic and focused. Much of what we consider as individual based leadership undergoes a change to building systems (even as subtle as a meeting dynamics), that elevate.

The suggestive nature, not prescriptive by any means, lends itself easily to reading and assimilation. A must read for all leaders, managers and individual contributors across levels. My ask of the readers is to read one chapter at a time.

Kudos, dear Suresh.

S V Nathan, Author, Speaker and ex CHRO & Partner of Deloitte South Asia

In my role as an enterprise CFO, I've learned that the hardest leadership shift is stepping back at the right moments. *Lead Less, Build More* captures this concept with clarity and honesty, showing how organizations scale best when leaders focus less on control and more on building systems, trust, and clear decision rights.

The book is practical and based on real life experiences, not theory. The book addresses the realities of leading at scale. A thoughtful read for leaders who want their organizations to perform well even when they are not in the room.

Jiten Shah, CFO - RSM US LLP

Acknowledgement

If *Lead Less, Build More* has a beginning, it didn't start with a book proposal or a writing plan.

It started with a conversation.

K S Ramanan, an ex-colleague and a friend, planted the first inconvenient question: "Why don't you write?"
Not because I had something urgent to say, but because writing, he believed, would help me make sense of what I already knew but hadn't yet articulated. He was right. Reflection, it turns out, is a leadership skill hiding in plain sight.

That spark turned into discipline when Shailendra Saxena, Partner at Ernst & Young, pushed me to write systematically—every week, without drama. That cadence gave birth to the LinkedIn newsletter **It Is What It Is**. And without that structure, this book would still be an idea waiting for the "right time." Quite simply, without these two gentlemen, this book would not exist.

Another moment stayed with me longer than I expected.

During a storytelling workshop at Indian School of Business, Ameen Haque posed a deceptively simple question: "If you don't tell your story, who will?"

That line kept replaying in my mind. It slowly shifted writing from an exercise into a responsibility—and ultimately became the quiet push behind this book.

Long before newsletters and chapters, my leadership thinking was shaped by people who taught me not what to think, but how to think.

At Shaw Wallace, the late K. Srinivasan introduced me to purpose-driven leadership and lateral thinking—not as theory, but as a practical way of navigating ambiguity when straight lines fail.

H. N. Subba Rao, former Director of Texmaco, encouraged me to think like an engineer: break problems down, respect constraints, and design for reality. That mindset permanently expanded my finance lens.

My journey at Ernst & Young began in an airport lounge in Mumbai. Haren Bhat didn't just induct me into the firm—he taught me how to speak my mind with clarity and conviction. A rare skill in environments that often reward politeness over honesty.

At the firm's highest levels, Jim Turley, former Chairman and CEO of EY, demonstrated that values are not statements on walls; they are choices made when trade-offs are real. Watching him lead was a masterclass in integrity without theatrics.

Mike Ventling, former CFO of EY, reinforced a lesson leaders often learn too late: decisions taken for the right cause age far better than those taken for convenience. His influence shaped my understanding of courage in leadership and finance alike.

During one of the most critical transformation journeys of my career, Dinesh Pai showed me what bold decision-making looks like in practice—calm, decisive, and anchored in conviction rather than noise. That experience changed how I show up when the stakes are high.

This book was also shaped by a group of thoughtful beta readers who engaged deeply with early drafts. They challenged assumptions, surfaced blind spots, questioned what felt obvious to me, and helped sharpen what truly needed clarity. Their collective generosity of time and intellect made this manuscript stronger.

I am grateful to Ramesh Shankar, Srikanth Dwarkanath, Anton Musgrave, Haren Bhat, Nathan SV, Prarit Batra, Subramanian Ananthakrishnan and Shailendra Saxena for that role.

A special word of thanks to Shiv Shenoy, who partnered with me through this journey—offering candid feedback, asking uncomfortable questions, and helping shape the book as both a thinking partner and a steady sounding board.

I would also like to thank Abhijit Bharatkumar, my son-in-law, who contributed significantly to the overall structure and design of the book, especially the cartoon ideas that bring many of these concepts to life.

Each of these individuals shaped my leadership journey in ways they may not fully realize.

This book is not a tribute to them—it is evidence of their influence.

And if leadership is about building systems that outlast individuals, then *Lead Less, Build More* stands on foundations laid quietly, generously, and without expectation of credit.

Content

Foreword v

Practitioner Perspective vi

Academic Perspective viii

Reactions to Lead Less, Build More x

Acknowledgement xiv

Prologue xix

Part 1 Letting go : From Heroics to Intent 1

Chapter 1   The Art of Doing Nothing 3

Chapter 2   The Leadership Reset 23

Chapter 3   Trust is the Operating System 49

Chapter 4   Hierarchy Doesn't Guarantee Results 75

Part 2 Building What Lasts : Systems that work without you 95

Chapter 5   Listening Is A Leadership Superpower 97

Chapter 6   Clarity over Consensus 119

Chapter 7   Conflict as a Competitive Advantage 139

Chapter 8   Ownership That Scales 157

Chapter 9   Decisions at Speed 173

Chapter 10 The Audacity Operating System 191

Part 3 Sustaining the Future : Leadership Beyond Presence 209

Chapter 11 AI as Co-Leader.. 211

Chapter 12 From Silos to Pods... 231

Chapter 13 Change That Sticks.. 253

A quiet companion to Lead Less, Build More 281

Epilogue.. 285

The Thinking Behind the Book 292

Bibliography... 295

Prologue

Lead Less, Build More – An Invitation to Sustainable Leadership

Every book begins with an idea. This one began with a realization.

For years, I watched leaders work harder, talk louder, and run faster…yet struggle to move their organizations forward. They carried every problem on their shoulders, mistaking personal heroism for impact.

Somewhere along the way, leadership had become synonymous with doing everything.

Then, during a conversation with a client, I heard myself say, almost without thinking:

"You don't scale by doing more. You scale by designing systems that don't need you to do everything."

That sentence stayed with me.

It wasn't about detachment or delegation. It was about trust — trusting people, processes, and principles enough to let them work without your constant supervision.

That moment became the seed for this book.

The Genesis of a Reflection

I didn't write this book to glorify leadership. I wrote it to liberate it.

I've seen what happens when capable, well-meaning leaders become the bottleneck to their own success. They build high-performance teams that still wait for approval, create strong organizations that still need rescuing, and deliver brilliant results that disappear once they leave.

> *Leadership that can't outlive the leader isn't leadership—it is dependency disguised as dedication.*

This book is about the opposite kind of power—the kind that builds systems strong enough to stand without you, cultures that sustain momentum without your daily push, and people who grow not because you control them, but because you trust them.

The Paradox of Leadership

We were all raised to believe that great leaders lead more—decide more, know more, do more. But every organization I've seen thrive over time has one thing in common: leaders who lead less so that others can build more.

They understand that leadership isn't an act of control; it's an act of creation. They don't just chase results; they design environments where results happen naturally.

> *Leadership, I've learned, is not about being indispensable. It's about being unnecessary in the right places.*

What This Book Is (and Isn't)

This is not a book of management hacks or quick wins. It's a collection of lessons about scaling trust, designing systems, and building organizations that don't collapse when the leader takes a vacation.

You'll find reflections on clarity, conflict, ownership, courage, speed, and change—the hidden architecture of systems that scale. Each chapter comes from real places—from finance transformations, global projects, mentoring sessions, and quiet moments when I realized that letting go often achieves more than holding on.

Think of this book less as a manual and more as a blueprint not for control, but for continuity.

The Journey You're About to Begin

The book unfolds in three parts:

Part One explores the inner shift required to lead less: the mindset change from hero to architect. You'll discover why doing nothing can create clarity, why hierarchy doesn't guarantee results, and how listening becomes your superpower.

Part Two moves into the mechanics of how to design systems that clarify, empower, and self-correct. You'll learn why clarity beats consensus, how to harness constructive conflict (an ancient concept called *Tharkam*), how to make decisions at speed, and how to create ownership structures that multiply rather than centralize.

Part Three looks ahead on how technology, AI, and culture shape the future of scalable leadership. You'll explore AI as a co-leader rather than just a tool, how to move from silos to pod-based structures, and most importantly, how to make change stick when everyone's exhausted by transformation.

It ends, fittingly, with a mountain, because some lessons about leading less can only be learned by climbing.

If the chapters before that are about how to lead, the final one is about how to be.

A Final Invitation

If you've ever felt the exhaustion of carrying everything yourself, this book permits you to step back without stepping out.

Leading less isn't abdication. It's evolution. At some point, you stop controlling and start clarifying, stop hovering and start building systems, and stop being everywhere to signal involvement.

The greatest leaders don't leave legacies of dependence. They leave frameworks that others can build on.

Because the true measure of leadership is not how much you lead while you're present, but how well things work when you're not.

Part 1
Letting go : From Heroics to Intent

Chapter 1
The Art of Doing Nothing

"This was the original FOMO – "Fear Of Missing One more notification."

The Collapse

The email arrived at around 2 AM. I know the exact time because I was awake to see it.

I'd been awake at 2 AM for the past six nights, staring at my laptop screen in a hotel room in Frankfurt, trying to fix a problem that probably could have waited until morning. Probably. But in that moment, with my mind running on fumes and adrenaline, everything felt urgent. Everything felt like it needed my immediate attention.

The email was from my CEO. Subject line: "Quick question."

I clicked it open, read three sentences asking about a metric I'd sent him two weeks ago, and spent the next forty minutes crafting a response. Not because it was complicated—it wasn't—but because my brain had become so scattered that even simple tasks required Herculean effort.

I hit send at 3:31 AM and closed my laptop with a grim sense of accomplishment. I'd been productive. I'd been responsive. I'd been everything a senior executive should be.

I was also, as I would discover six weeks later, completely burning out.

The wake-up call came during a routine leadership meeting. My CFO was presenting quarterly forecasts when I realized I couldn't follow what he was saying. Not because the content was complex, since I had sat through hundreds of these presentations before, but because my brain simply couldn't process the information. Words washed over me like white noise. I nodded at appropriate moments, but I was intellectually absent.

After the meeting, I locked myself in my office and stared at the wall for twenty minutes. Not intentionally. I simply couldn't summon the energy to do anything else. My calendar showed seven more meetings that day. The thought of attending them filled me with a profound exhaustion that went beyond physical tiredness.

That's when I understood: I'd been operating at maximum capacity for so long that I'd forgotten what normal felt like. I'd confused motion with progress, busyness with effectiveness, and relentless availability with leadership.

I'd forgotten how to stop.

The Busyness Trap

If you've spent any time in corporate leadership, you've witnessed the peculiar arms race of busyness. Someone mentions they worked until 9 PM, someone else tops them with a weekend spent answering emails, and before long, exhaustion becomes a badge of honor.

I've sat in executive meetings where leaders competed over who had less sleep, who travelled more, who went longer without a real vacation. I wore burnout like medals, proof of our commitment and value to the organization.

The logic seemed airtight: more hours meant more output meant more value. If I could just push harder, work longer, respond faster, I'd break through to the next level of performance.

But something fundamental was broken in that equation, and I was living proof.

Research from the World Health Organization found that working more than 55 hours per week increases the risk of stroke by 35% and heart disease by 17%. But the damage isn't just physical. Stanford economist John Pencavel's research showed that productivity per hour declines sharply after 50 hours per week, and drops off so dramatically after 55 hours that there's literally no point in working more.

In other words, the extra hours we're grinding out don't just harm us. They produce almost nothing of value

Research consistently shows that working fewer hours with strategic breaks often increases output rather than decreasing it—sometimes dramatically. The results shouldn't be surprising. They align with decades of research showing that human beings aren't designed for sustained, unbroken cognitive effort. Our brains need cycles of exertion and recovery. Push too hard for too long, and the system starts breaking down in ways that are invisible until the damage is severe.

I learned this the hard way during my burnout period. I was producing more emails, attending more meetings, and making more decisions than ever before. But the quality of everything I touched had deteriorated. I was making errors in judgment I would have caught easily six months earlier. I was missing opportunities that should have been obvious. I was present in body but increasingly absent in mind.

Here's what nobody tells you about relentless busyness. Over time, it doesn't just make you less effective; it narrows what you're capable of seeing.

When you're always in execution mode, always responding to the next urgent item, you lose the ability to think strategically. You become reactive rather than proactive. You optimize for today's crisis at the expense of next year's opportunity.

I saw this clearly with one of my direct reports, a brilliant operations leader I'll call Marcus. Marcus was legendary for his responsiveness. Email him at any hour, and you'd get a reply within minutes. Need something done urgently? Marcus was your person.

But over the course of a year, I watched Marcus's strategic thinking atrophy. In meetings, he'd dive straight into tactical details without stepping back to question whether we were solving the right problem. He'd volunteer for every urgent project but never had time to think about the structural improvements that could prevent those urgent projects from existing in the first place.

Chapter 1
The Art of Doing Nothing

When I finally sat him down for a difficult conversation, he was genuinely surprised. "I thought I was doing exactly what you needed," he said. "I'm always available. I'm always delivering."

"You are," I told him. "But you're so busy delivering that you've stopped thinking about what we should be delivering in the first place."

That conversation changed how I thought about my own patterns. If I could see Marcus's over-commitment eroding his strategic value, what was my own relentless pace doing to mine?

The Science of Strategic Pauses

The breakthrough in my understanding came not from management literature but from neuroscience research on something called the Default Mode Network (DMN).

The DMN activates when your mind isn't locked onto a task. Those moments when you're staring out a window, showering, or lying in bed before sleep are when it switches on.

For decades, researchers thought this was your brain idling. But Marcus Raichle's ground-breaking work at Washington University showed the DMN does some of your brain's most important cognitive work.

The DMN integrates information from different experiences, makes unexpected connections between disparate ideas, consolidates learning, and processes emotional experiences. It's during DMN activation that insights emerge, that the solution to a problem you've been wrestling with suddenly becomes clear, that you see patterns you'd been missing.

In other words, the moments when you think you're doing nothing are often the moments when your brain is doing its most valuable work.

But here's the catch: the DMN only activates when you stop actively focusing on tasks. As long as you're in execution mode...answering emails, attending meetings, working through your to-do list—you're suppressing the very network that generates insights and strategic thinking.

This explained something I'd noticed but never understood: my best ideas rarely came at my desk. They emerged during my morning run, in the shower, on a flight when I'd forgotten to download work files and was forced to stare out the window for two hours.

I wasn't just getting lucky during these moments. I was giving my brain permission to do the kind of thinking that's impossible during constant task execution.

The practical implications became clear when I discovered research validating the Pomodoro Technique: work for 25 minutes, break for 5. Repeat. Every four cycles, take a longer 15-30 minute break.

What seemed like a simple time-management hack turned out to align perfectly with how the brain actually works. Research by Nathaniel Kleitman and others showed that humans operate on 90-120 minute ultradian rhythms—cycles of high and low alertness. Within those cycles, we can sustain peak focus for about 25-50 minutes before our attention starts to drift.

Fighting that drift is exhausting and ineffective. Working with it—building in regular breaks that let your attention restore—is dramatically more productive.

When I finally started implementing structured breaks into my own work pattern, the results were immediate. Not because I was working more hours—I was working fewer—but because the hours I worked were dramatically more focused and the breaks gave my DMN time to process and integrate.

Chapter 1
The Art of Doing Nothing

I started solving problems I'd been stuck on for weeks. I began seeing patterns in our business that I'd been too close to notice. And perhaps most importantly, I stopped making the kind of exhaustion-driven errors that had been creeping into my work.

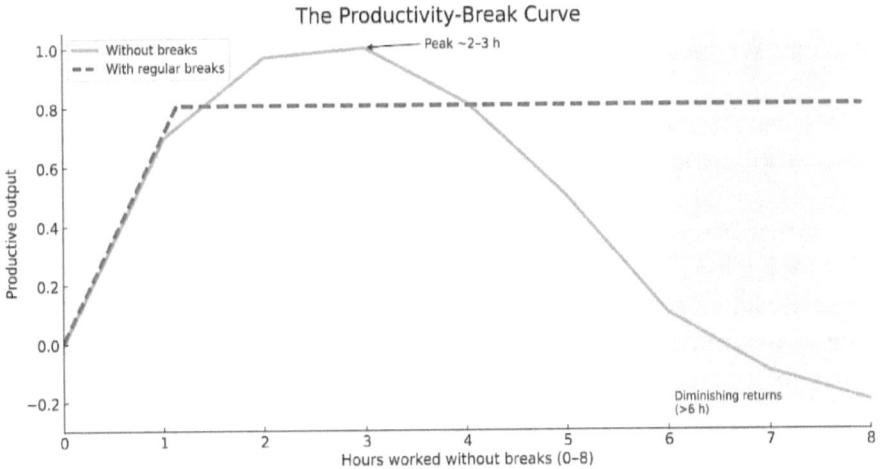

Productivity without breaks peaks early and declines rapidly. Regular strategic pauses maintain consistent high-quality output.

When Doing Nothing Saved Everything

Let me tell you about the moment when stepping back saved a $50 million deal.

We were three months into negotiations with a potential acquisition target. The deal made strategic sense: they had technology we needed, we had distribution channels they lacked, the financials worked. But something felt off. I couldn't articulate what, exactly. The data all looked good. Due diligence hadn't raised any red flags. My team was enthusiastic.

But in my gut, something didn't sit right.

The problem was, I couldn't justify my hesitation with data. And in a room full of analytical executives, gut feelings don't carry much weight. My CFO was pushing hard to close. Our board was eager. The target company was getting impatient.

I was scheduled to present our final recommendation to the board on a Thursday. On the Tuesday before, feeling the pressure mounting, I did something I'd never done before in a high-stakes situation: I blocked off my entire Wednesday calendar. All of it. No meetings. No calls. No email.

My assistant thought I was sick. My team was confused—we had a board presentation in 48 hours. But I held firm.

I spent that Wednesday doing what most executives would consider nothing. I took a long morning walk. I sat in a park and watched people. I had a leisurely lunch alone. I took a nap in the afternoon—something I hadn't done on a workday in probably a decade. I went for an evening run. I read a novel before bed.

No work. No thinking about the acquisition. Just genuine mental space.

Thursday morning, I woke up at 5 AM with absolute clarity. The problem wasn't with the technology or the financials. It was with the culture. The target company had a top-down, command-and-control culture that would be toxic when integrated with our more collaborative approach. I'd seen the signs during our meetings—the way their CEO shut down questions, the way their team looked to him before answering anything—but I'd been too busy processing information to register what it meant.

I called an emergency meeting with my executive team. I explained what I'd realized. Initially, they pushed back—culture issues seemed squishy compared to the hard-financial benefits. But as we talked through the implications, they started seeing it too. We'd been so focused on the technical integration that we'd glossed over the human one.

We restructured the deal. Instead of a full acquisition, we negotiated a technology licensing agreement with partnership options. It took longer. It was less sexy. But it protected us from a cultural integration nightmare that would have destroyed value for years.

That Wednesday of "doing nothing" saved us from what I'm convinced would have been a disastrous acquisition. More importantly, it taught me something fundamental about how I work: my best strategic thinking doesn't happen at my desk. It happens when I step away from my desk and give my mind space to process.

The Manager's Toolkit: Strategic Pauses in Practice

After my burnout experience and that critical Wednesday, I became obsessed with understanding how to systematically integrate pauses into leadership work. Here's what actually works:

Tool 1: The Morning Mental Buffer

Most leaders start their day reactive—checking email, responding to overnight messages, diving straight into problems. This sets a pattern of reactivity that lasts all day.

I now protect the first 30 minutes of every workday as a mental buffer. No email. No Slack. No news. I use it variably: sometimes a walk, sometimes sitting with coffee and letting my mind wander, sometimes light reading unrelated to work.

The impact is subtle but profound. Instead of starting the day in response mode, I start it with intention. I think about what actually matters today. I notice patterns from the previous day that I was too busy to register. I enter my first meeting grounded rather than reactive.

Implementation note: Start with 10 minutes if 30 feels impossible. Put it on your calendar as "Strategic Thinking Time." Don't defend it; just do it consistently. After two weeks, you'll have enough evidence of its value to justify protecting it.

Tool 2: The Inter-Meeting Pause

Back-to-back meetings are productivity poison. You're processing the previous meeting while trying to engage with the current one, doing justice to neither.

I now enforce a 5-minute buffer between all meetings. If someone sends me a meeting invitation from 2:00-3:00, I accept it but block my calendar from 1:55-2:00 and 3:00-3:05.

Those five minutes before each meeting let me mentally close the previous topic and prepare for the next one. The five minutes after let me capture key insights while they're fresh and decide on any immediate actions.

The practice: During these pauses, I don't check email or messages. I either sit quietly, take a brief walk, or jot notes on the meeting just concluded. That's it.

Tool 3: The Weekly Reset

Every Friday afternoon, I block 90 minutes for what I call a Weekly Reset. No meetings. Phone on silent. Door closed.

I use this time to:

- Review what actually got accomplished versus what I planned
- Identify patterns in how I spent my time
- Note problems or opportunities that emerged during the week
- Think about whether I'm focused on the right priorities

This isn't just planning next week's calendar—it's stepping back to think about whether I'm working on what matters. Some of my biggest strategic shifts have emerged from Friday Reset sessions.

Tool 4: The Quarterly Offline Day

Four times a year, I take an entire day completely offline. No email, no phone, no Slack. I tell my team I'm available for genuine emergencies (hospital-level crises), but otherwise unreachable.

I spend these days thinking about the big questions:

- Are we solving the right problems?
- What are we missing?
- Where should we be investing more energy?
- What should we stop doing?

These questions are impossible to answer in the flow of daily work. They require sustained, uninterrupted thinking that's only possible when you completely unplug.

The results: At least half of my most impactful strategic decisions have emerged from or been refined during Quarterly Offline Days. The ROI on 4 days per year is extraordinary.

Tool 5: The Forced Boredom Exercise

This one sounds ridiculous, but it's powerful: deliberately engineer boredom into your routine.

Take the stairs instead of the elevator, but don't check your phone during the climb. Wait in line at the coffee shop without scrolling through messages. Sit in your car for five minutes before heading into the office, doing nothing.

These micro-moments of boredom train your brain to be comfortable with stillness. They break the addiction to constant stimulation. And often, during these moments, insights emerge.

I've solved nagging problems while waiting for my coffee to brew, made important connections during a flight delay I couldn't fill with work, and clarified strategic direction during an enforced five-minute wait in a building lobby.

The boredom itself isn't the goal—it's the mental state that boredom creates. When your brain isn't fed constant external input, it starts generating its own. Often, what it generates is exactly what you need.

Building a Culture That Values Pause

Individual practices are important, but if you're a leader, your real leverage is in shaping organizational culture. Here's the uncomfortable truth: your team will never feel safe taking pauses if you don't model it and explicitly encourage it.

When I first started implementing structured breaks, I kept them private. I didn't want to seem like I was slacking while everyone else was grinding. But that privacy meant my team never saw that breaks were acceptable, let alone valuable.

The shift came when I started being explicit. In team meetings, I'd mention, "I spent Wednesday offline thinking about our Q3 strategy." When someone sent me a great idea, I'd ask, "Where were you when this came to you?" More often than not: in the shower, on a walk, driving home.

I started actively celebrating these moments. "That insight about the customer segment—you got that during your run? That's exactly why I protect my morning walks. Good thinking requires space."

The message landed. Within a quarter, team members started protecting their own thinking time. They'd mention they were blocking Friday mornings for deep work. They'd suggest walking meetings instead of conference room discussions. The culture shifted from busyness-as-virtue to thoughtfulness-as-virtue.

One of the most impactful cultural changes was reforming our meeting structure:

The 45-minute meeting default: We shifted from 60-minute to 45-minute meetings as the default. Those 15 minutes gave everyone mental transition time.

Walking 1-on-1s: For any 1-on-1 that didn't require screen-sharing, we defaulted to walking meetings. Different physical state, different cognitive state, better conversations.

No-meeting Thursdays: We designated Thursdays as meeting-free days. Anyone could block their entire Thursday for deep work or reflective thinking. The first month, people didn't know what to do with themselves. By month three, Thursday had become our most productive day.

The 48-hour email rule: We established a norm that emails sent after 6 PM or on weekends didn't require same-day responses. Response within 48 hours was fine. This simple rule dramatically reduced the anxiety of constant availability.

The Microsoft Story: When Strategic Pauses Scale

The most compelling evidence for organization-wide pause practices comes from Microsoft's Japan experiment. In August 2019, Microsoft Japan gave all 2,300 employees every Friday off for a month. They called it the "Work-Life Choice Challenge." Offices were closed. Meetings were prohibited. Employees were encouraged to use the time as they saw fit..

The results shocked even the optimists:

- Productivity (measured by sales per employee) increased 39.9%
- Employees printed 58.7% fewer pages
- Electricity costs decreased 23.1%
- 92.1% of employees reported satisfaction with the program

But the quantitative results weren't the most interesting part. The qualitative feedback revealed something deeper: employees reported feeling more creative, more energized, and more strategic in their thinking. With the forced break, they stopped filling time with busywork and focused on what actually mattered.

One manager reported: "I realized that most of what I did on Fridays wasn't actually necessary. When I came back to a four-day week, I was much more ruthless about priorities."

The experiment revealed something that should be obvious but gets lost in hustle culture: time at work and productive output are not the same thing. Often, they're inversely related.

Everything I've described assumes you have control over your schedule. But what if you're a middle manager in an organization that worships busyness? What if your boss sends emails at midnight and expects responses? What if your company culture actively punishes anything that looks like "taking it easy"?

This is the reality for many managers, and it requires a different approach.

The Stealth Break

You don't need to announce your break strategy to benefit from it. You can implement personal pause practices without making them visible:

The bathroom strategy: Take a 5-minute walk to a bathroom on a different floor. Use those minutes to close your eyes and breathe. No one questions bathroom breaks.

The "coffee run" reset: Instead of making coffee at your desk, walk to a café two blocks away. Use the walk as thinking time.

Chapter 1
The Art of Doing Nothing

The early arrival buffer: Come to the office 30 minutes before your official start time. Use those minutes for your morning mental buffer. You're technically "at work," so no one can complain, but you're protecting thinking time.

The calendar block technique: Block thinking time on your calendar with generic labels: "Project planning," "Strategic review," "Prep time." People see a blocked calendar and assume you're busy. Use the time for reflective pauses.

The ROI Conversation

If you want to be more explicit about needing thinking time, frame it in terms your organization values: return on investment.

One manager I coached, Lauren, worked in a brutal always-on consulting environment. She wanted to protect Friday mornings for strategic thinking but knew her managing director would see it as slacking.

Her approach: she tracked her work for a month and identified that her highest-value deliverables—the insights that clients actually paid for—came from deep, uninterrupted thinking sessions, not from the constant fire-fighting and email responsiveness that filled her days.

She presented her managing director with data: "My analysis shows that the three client insights that generated follow-on work this quarter all emerged from focused thinking time. I'd like to test blocking Friday mornings for this kind of work. I'll measure the results against my current output and report back in a month."

Framed as an experiment with measurable outcomes, her MD approved. Within that month, Sarah produced two major insights that led to contract extensions. The Friday morning blocks became permanent and eventually spread to her team.

The lesson: don't ask for permission to work less. Propose an experiment to work smarter, with clear metrics for success.

You're not alone in feeling overwhelmed by constant busyness. Others in your organization are likely struggling with the same issues. Find them. Build alliances.

Start a "Strategic Thinking Circle" where a small group meets monthly to discuss insights from your pause practices. Share what you're learning. Create accountability. Celebrate wins.

When multiple people start producing better strategic work and attributing it to structured thinking time, it becomes harder for the organization to ignore. Culture change often starts from the middle, not the top.

The Path Back from Burnout

Let me return to where I started: my own burnout and what brought me back.

After that leadership meeting where I couldn't process basic financial information, I knew something had to change. I couldn't sustain the pace I'd been running. But I also couldn't just stop—I had responsibilities, a team counting on me, targets to hit.

The path back wasn't dramatic. It was incremental. I started with the smallest possible change: a 10-minute morning walk before checking email.

The first few days felt absurd. But I committed to two weeks. By day four, I felt a shift. The brief pause helped me reconnect with what actually mattered before urgency took over again.

After two weeks, I extended it to 20 minutes. Then I added 5-minute breaks between meetings. Then Friday afternoon reset sessions. Small, sustainable changes that accumulated into a fundamentally different way of working.

Three months later, I had my energy back. Six months later, my strategic thinking had sharpened noticeably. A year later, I couldn't imagine working any other way.

The most unexpected result: I was working fewer hours but producing better work. My team was more effective because I was more present when I engaged with them. Board meetings went better because I'd actually thought about the business instead of just reacting to it.

I learned something that sounds paradoxical but is absolutely true: sometimes the most productive thing you can do is nothing at all.

Actions for Readers: Your Pause Practice

If you're feeling the pull of constant busyness, if you're recognizing patterns of burnout in your own work, here's how to start building pauses into your leadership practice:

This Week: Start Small

1. Block the first 15 minutes of your workday. No email, no meetings, no Slack. Walk, sip coffee quietly, or just think. Five consecutive days. Track how you feel.

2. Add 5-minute meeting buffers. For every meeting on your calendar this week, protect 5 minutes before and after. Use those minutes to transition mentally. Notice the difference in your focus.

3. Take one deliberate boredom break. When you're waiting (elevator, line, etc.), resist checking your phone. Just be. Notice what your mind does when it's not fed constant input.

This Month: Build the Framework

4. Establish your weekly reset. Block 60-90 minutes on Friday afternoon (or whatever day works) for reflection and strategic thinking. Make it recurring. Protect it like you'd protect a meeting with your CEO.

5. Try a walking 1-on-1. Next time you have a 1-on-1 that doesn't require screensharing, suggest a walk. Pay attention to how the conversation differs.

6. Track your insights. Keep a simple log of when your best ideas come to you. Meeting? Desk work? Shower? Commute? After a month, you'll have data showing when your brain does its best thinking.

This Quarter: Transform Your Practice

7. Schedule your first quarterly offline day. Block a full day in the next three months. Unavailable except for genuine emergencies. Spend it thinking about big-picture questions. Return with at least one strategic shift.

8. Have the ROI conversation (if needed). Track the value of insights that emerge from your pause practices. Share results with your manager if you need organizational buy-in.

9. Build your alliance. Find 2-3 colleagues interested in working smarter. Start a monthly strategic thinking circle. Share practices, insights, and accountability.

A Final Story

I'll leave you with one more moment from my journey.

Six months into my new pause practices, I attended an industry conference. At the networking dinner, I ended up at a table with several other executives. The conversation turned, inevitably, to how busy everyone was.

Chapter 1
The Art of Doing Nothing

"I haven't had a real weekend in two months," one CEO said.

"I was answering emails until 2 AM last night," another added.

"I can't remember the last time I took a full vacation," a third contributed.

They looked at me, expecting a similar story. Instead, I said, "I blocked yesterday afternoon for thinking time. Spent two hours offline. Solved a problem we'd been stuck on for three weeks."

The table went quiet. Then one of the CEOs said, "You can do that?"

"Not only can I do it," I replied, "I can't afford not to. The cost of constant busyness was my strategic thinking. The investment in pause practices gave it back."

That conversation led to three follow-up discussions, two consulting engagements helping other companies build pause practices, and a speaking invitation to share these ideas more broadly.

But more importantly, it confirmed something I'd come to believe: we're not alone in drowning in busyness. We're not alone in sensing that relentless hustle is counterproductive. And we're not alone in discovering that pauses aren't a luxury—they're essential to doing our best work.

The art of doing nothing isn't about working less. It's about working better. It's about creating the mental space where insight emerges, where strategy clarifies, where you reconnect with what actually matters.

In a world that never stops moving, the leaders who create space to pause are the ones who see furthest and move most effectively.

Your next strategic breakthrough might not come from working harder. It might come from the courage to stop, breathe, and let your mind do what it does best when you finally give it room to think.

Chapter 2
The Leadership Reset

"EVER HEARD OF DELEGATION?"

The Hero's Trap

The call came at 8 PM on a Tuesday. Our client delivery manager, voice tight with stress: "We have a problem. The client just doubled their resource requirements. They need 150 people in six weeks, not 75 in twelve. And they're threatening to pull the contract if we can't deliver."

Lead Less, Build More

I was in the middle of dinner with my family. My daughter was telling me about her school play. But the moment I heard "threatening to pull the contract," the rest of the world went mute. This was a $12 million account. Losing it would crater our quarterly numbers and damage our reputation in the market.

"I'll handle it," I said, already mentally cataloguing who I needed to call. "Set up a war room meeting for 7 AM tomorrow."

I spent that night drafting recruitment strategies, texting agency contacts, mapping out accelerated hiring workflows. By morning, I had a plan. By the 7 AM meeting, I was ready to take charge.

The HR head admitted their team wasn't equipped for this kind of surge hiring. Their processes were built for steady-state recruitment, not emergency scaling. Their agency relationships were thin. The capacity simply wasn't there.

That was my cue. Every instinct I'd honed over two decades of leadership kicked in. This was what I did. This was what made me valuable. I would fix it.

I took over the recruitment drive personally. I negotiated with agencies, bypassed standard approval workflows, made rapid-fire decisions on salary bands and offer letters. I worked sixteen-hour days for three weeks, fueled by coffee, adrenaline, and the conviction that the organization needed me to be the hero.

And it worked. Within six weeks, we'd staffed the project. The client was satisfied. The contract was saved. In the executive meeting the following Monday, the CEO said what I'd heard countless times before: "Suresh saved the day."

It felt good. Familiar. Validating. Another crisis averted, another fire extinguished, another proof that I was indispensable.

Chapter 2
The Leadership Reset

In that moment of victory, I couldn't see the deeper damage I had just caused..

The Pattern I Couldn't See

Three months later, we faced another urgent hiring need. Different client, similar pressure. And once again, the same pattern emerged: HR struggled, I intervened, the problem got solved, everyone breathed easier.

But this time, in a quiet moment after the crisis passed, someone on my leadership team said something that landed differently than it should have.

"We need more people like Suresh."

Usually, I'd smile. Feel a surge of pride. Take it as the compliment it was intended to be. But that day, for reasons I couldn't immediately articulate, the words felt wrong.

More people like Suresh.

I sat with that phrase for a while. Turned it over. Examined it from different angles.

What would "more Sureshes" actually mean for the organization?

Would it mean we'd be stronger or just better at firefighting?

Would it mean we'd have built systems that worked without constant intervention—or just more heroes jumping into recurring crises?

Would it mean the next generation of leaders were developing their own capacity or learning to wait for someone to rescue them?

The more I thought about it, the more uncomfortable I became. Because the pattern was clear once I stopped admiring my own heroics long enough to see it:

Every time I "saved the day," I prevented the organization from building the capacity to save itself.

Every time I jumped in, I reinforced the message that systems didn't need to improve because Suresh would fix it.

Every time I became indispensable, I made the organization more fragile.

I'd spent twenty years building a reputation as the person who could handle anything. What I'd actually built was a sophisticated form of organizational dependency.

As I started examining my leadership patterns more critically, **I realized I'd been relying on three fundamental levers: title, control, and consensus.** They'd served me well early in my career. They'd helped me advance, gain influence, and build credibility.

But somewhere along the way, they'd stopped working. Or more accurately, they had started working against me and against the organization's ability to function without my constant intervention.

Title: The Authority That Wasn't

For years, my title gave me comfort. VP Finance opened doors. It got me into important meetings. It meant people listened when I spoke. Title felt like power.

But the longer I led, the more I noticed a troubling pattern: the people who actually moved the organization forward often had the least impressive titles.

Chapter 2
The Leadership Reset

I watched a mid-level analyst in one of our planning meetings ask a simple question that completely reframed a debate that had been spinning for weeks. No authority. No formal power. Just clarity. Within five minutes, the entire executive team had pivoted to her perspective.

Meanwhile, I'd seen senior leaders with impressive titles struggle to get their teams to execute even straightforward initiatives. The title commanded deference in meetings, but it didn't translate to action afterward.

Paul Polman's transformation of Unilever crystallized this for me. When he became CEO in 2009, he had all the positional authority needed. But the culture was risk-averse and short-term focused. Polman didn't try to fix this through organizational mandates. He reframed leadership around long-term purpose and sustainability, modeling behavior rather than commanding it. The shift wasn't about title. It was about behavior.

My title might get me into the room. But it wouldn't make anyone trust my judgment, execute my ideas, or believe in the direction I set.

In today's organizations, especially with knowledge workers, people don't follow titles anymore.

They follow whoever reduces uncertainty without destroying honesty. They follow clarity, not hierarchy.

Control: The Quality Mirage

If title was my first crutch, control was my second. For years, I believed more oversight meant better outcomes. More approval gates, more reviews, more sign-offs.

I was wrong. Every additional layer slowed decisions, filtered truth, and made problems more expensive to fix. Teams learned to manage the reporting process instead of the actual work. Status updates became theatre.

The breakthrough in my understanding came from studying Alan Mulally's turnaround of Ford. When Mulally arrived as CEO in 2006, Ford was hemorrhaging billions. The company had layers upon layers of controls, endless review meetings, elaborate reporting structures, complex approval chains.

But none of it was producing quality. It was producing cover.

Mulally introduced a simple weekly Business Plan Review where every leader reported progress in front of their peers using a straightforward color code: green for on-track, yellow for at-risk, red for trouble.

The first few weeks, everything was green. The company was losing $17 billion, but according to the dashboard, everything was fine.

Then one executive, Mark Fields, marked his launch of the Edge as red. The room went silent. This was career suicide in Ford's political culture.

Mulally's response changed everything: he applauded.

That single gesture rewired the culture. Red wasn't failure—red was truth. And truth was where quality begins. Within weeks, the dashboards reflected reality. Problems surfaced earlier. Solutions came faster. The culture shifted from defensive reporting to honest problem-solving.

I recognized my own pattern in Ford's pre-Mulally dysfunction. I'd built elaborate control systems that gave me the illusion of oversight but actually just delayed bad news and slowed response time.

Real quality doesn't come from more controls. It comes from clarity about what matters, fast feedback loops, and psychological safety to tell the truth early.

Chapter 2
The Leadership Reset

Consensus: The Comfort That Cost Us

The third lever, consensus, was the trickiest to recognize as a problem because it felt so virtuous.

When everyone in the room nods and agrees, it looks like alignment. It feels inclusive, collaborative, fair. Leaders who build consensus are praised for bringing people along, for not being autocratic, for valuing diverse perspectives.

But I learned through painful experience that consensus in the room often produces fragmentation in execution.

I'd leave meetings feeling great about the harmony we'd achieved, only to discover weeks later that different teams had interpreted the same "agreement" in completely different ways. We'd smile and nod together, then scatter into incoherent action.

Jack Welch had a similar insight. In one board meeting, his budget proposal sailed through without a single challenge. Instead of celebrating the smooth consensus, Welch stopped the meeting cold. "We're not moving forward until someone brings me a counterpoint," he insisted.

The next day, sharper debate exposed risks and improved the decision. Welch understood something I'd missed for years: polite agreement is worthless. What matters is whether people truly understand the decision, because execution depends on challenge, dissent, and clarity, not comfort

I'd been optimizing for comfort in meetings at the expense of clarity in execution. Consensus made me feel like a good leader. Clarity would have made me an effective one.

Leadership Models: Hero Trap vs Scalable Leadership

Hero trap
Lone leader dependency
Burnout risk
Scaling bottlenecks

Scalable leadership
Team empowerment
System-driven growth
Sustainable impact

The Cost of Heroics

The full cost of my hero complex became visible during a quarterly business review about six months after the second hiring crisis.

We were reviewing our operational metrics when the COO pulled up a troubling trend: our time-to-hire had actually gotten worse year-over-year, despite having gone through two major recruitment drives where we'd "proven" we could move fast.

Chapter 2
The Leadership Reset

"How is that possible?" I asked. "We hired 150 people in six weeks last quarter."

"We did," the COO said. "You did. But our standard process is still taking 90+ days for mid-level roles. Nothing has changed structurally."

The implication hung in the air. Every time I'd swooped in to save a hiring crisis, I'd prevented HR from confronting their broken process. They'd never had to build better agency relationships, streamline approvals, or invest in recruitment technology—because Suresh would handle it when it mattered.

I'd created a two-tier system: heroic intervention for crises, chronic dysfunction for everything else.

But the damage went deeper than HR's capability gap.

My own team had paid a price I'd been too busy to notice. While I was spending weeks managing recruitment for other functions, I wasn't fully leading my own. Strategic initiatives got delayed. Development conversations with my directs got postponed. I was so busy being a hero to other parts of the organization that I'd become an absentee leader to my own team.

The realization that my entire leadership model was broken was humbling. But as I started studying other leaders more carefully, I discovered something oddly comforting: even the greats had to reset.

Steve Jobs is the perfect example.

In his first stint at Apple, Jobs was the ultimate heroic leader. He dove into every detail, obsessed over control, defined himself by his ability to bend reality through sheer force of will. He was brilliant, visionary, and absolutely convinced that his intervention was necessary for anything important to succeed.

Lead Less, Build More

It worked—until it didn't. His need for control alienated the board and key executives. In 1985, he was forced out of the company he'd founded.

The Jobs who returned to Apple in 1997 was different. Still demanding, still visionary, but fundamentally transformed in how he led.

The second-era Jobs built systems, not just products. He recruited leaders like Tim Cook to run operations and Jony Ive to lead design, then trusted them to execute without his constant intervention. He created structures and processes that allowed brilliance to flourish without him being in every room.

His ambition didn't soften. It scaled. Because he learned to make the system the hero instead of himself.

General Stanley McChrystal went through a similar reset leading Joint Special Operations Command in Iraq. His instinct was tight command-and-control: strict hierarchy, centralized decision-making, clear chains of approval.

But Al Qaeda in Iraq was decentralized and moved fast. McChrystal's command structure was too slow. By the time intelligence reached headquarters, decisions were made, and orders flowed back to the field, the opportunity had passed.

McChrystal had to rethink his entire approach. He embraced "shared consciousness and empowered execution," ensuring context and clarity reached teams directly so they could move faster than centralized command ever allowed. He traded control for speed, hierarchy for networks.

The transformation worked. Not because his teams became more obedient, but because they became more autonomous.

Indra Nooyi admitted that her early leadership style at PepsiCo was combative and directive. She'd argue forcefully in meetings, make decisions quickly, and expect immediate execution. It was effective in the short term but exhausting for everyone and created a culture where people stopped bringing their full thinking because they knew Indra would override it anyway.

Over time, she reset. She leaned into listening, empathy, and genuine collaboration. Not because it was softer—because it was more sustainable. Influence, she discovered, lasts longer than authority.

The pattern across all these leaders was consistent: the most effective ones eventually traded the armor of heroics for the discipline of systems.

I wasn't alone in needing a reset. I was just later to the realization than I should have been.

The New Questions

After my realization, I took a week off. Not for vacation but for thinking.

I spent that week walking, sitting in coffee shops, staring at walls. No laptop. No email. Just the question that had been gnawing at me: If heroics weren't the answer, what was?

The old questions I'd been asking myself for twenty years were:

- "What problem can I solve next?"
- "How do I get everyone to agree?"
- "How do I make sure this is done right?"

These questions had shaped my entire approach to leadership. They'd made me valuable. They'd built my reputation. But they'd also made me the bottleneck.

By the end of that week, I'd started asking different questions:

Old Leadership Reflex	New Leadership Question
What problem can I solve next?	What conditions do I need to create so this problem never comes to me in the first place?
How do I get everyone to agree?	How do I make the decision clear enough that people can move forward even if we disagree?
How do I make sure this is done right?	How do I set intent and boundaries, then let judgment travel faster than me?

These questions didn't feed my ego. They didn't make me feel like a hero. They didn't generate immediate applause.

But they pointed toward something more valuable: building organizational capacity that would outlast my tenure and scale beyond my personal bandwidth.

The shift felt uncomfortable. It meant letting go of the very things that had defined my success. But the alternative—continuing to be indispensable—meant limiting the organization's growth to what I personally could handle.

That week of reflection marked the beginning of my leadership reset: from title, control, and consensus → to trust, clarity, ownership, and speed.

Theory is one thing. Practice is harder. The real reset came in moments when I had to override my instincts and act differently

Six months into my reset, I faced the perfect test.

Chapter 2
The Leadership Reset

Month-end close was approaching, and the finance team was behind. Their reconciliations weren't matching. Their processes were chaotic. The CFO was in panic mode.

My old instinct screamed at me: Jump in. You know how to fix this. You've done financial close reviews before. You can save them.

But I'd learned that every time I "saved" a team, I prevented them from building the capability to save themselves.

So, I did something that felt deeply uncomfortable: I didn't jump in.

Instead, I asked the finance lead three questions:

1. "What specific outcome do you need by month-end?" (Clarity over vagueness)
2. "Who on your team owns fixing this?" (Ownership over committees)
3. "What's preventing them from doing it?" (Systems over heroics)

The answers revealed the real problem: they didn't have a broken process, they had no process. Every month, different people handled close differently, using different templates, with different quality standards.

I resisted the urge to design the process for them. Instead, I said: "You have three weeks until the next close. I need you to design a standard process, train your team on it, and run a dry run by week two. I'll check in on progress, but this is yours to fix."

The finance lead looked terrified. "What if we mess it up?"

"Then we'll fix it together," I said. "But you'll own the process either way. I'm not going to rescue you monthly. . We're building capability, not creating dependency."

Those three weeks were hard. I had to sit on my hands while they struggled. I had to resist emails asking me to review their work. I had to trust they'd figure it out, or fail fast enough that we could learn and adjust.

They didn't fail. The process they designed was simpler and better than anything I would have created for them. More importantly, they owned it. When problems emerged in month two, they fixed them without escalating. By month three, close was running smoothly without any involvement from me.

The lesson: Every time you cover a gap, you teach the system it doesn't need to fix it.

The Product Launch: Clarity Under Pressure

Three months later, we had a major product launch approaching. Cross-functional teams—engineering, marketing, sales, operations—all had different ideas about what "ready to launch" meant.

In my old model, I would have run consensus meetings until everyone agreed. We'd have debated, wordsmithed, and negotiated until we could all nod together. It would have felt collaborative. It would have taken weeks. And we'd have left the room with different interpretations of what we'd "agreed" on.

Instead, I forced clarity.

In the launch review meeting, I wrote three things on the whiteboard:

1. **Outcome:** "Launch to beta customers by October 1, with 95% feature completeness and <3% critical bug rate."
2. **Boundaries:** "No new features after September 1. If we miss quality thresholds, we delay—no negotiation."

Chapter 2
The Leadership Reset

3. **Ownership:** "Rekha owns go/no-go decision. Engineering owns quality metrics. Marketing owns communication plan. If there's a conflict, Sarah makes the final call."

Someone immediately objected: "Shouldn't we all agree on when we're ready?"

"No," I said. "We should all be clear on the criteria and who decides. Agreement is optional. Clarity is mandatory."

We spent the next thirty minutes stress-testing the criteria. People argued. Some disagreed with the boundaries. A few thought Rekha was the wrong person to decide.

But by the end of the meeting, everyone could repeat back the same decision. We had clarity—not consensus.

The launch happened October 2 (we missed by a day due to a last-minute bug). But it succeeded because everyone knew what success meant and who owned what. No confusion. No drift. No post-meeting fragmentation into three different interpretations.

Consensus creates comfort in meetings.
Clarity creates results in the field.

The No List Revolution

By month nine of my reset, I'd learned that what you choose not to do is as important as what you choose to do.

Our annual planning session was approaching. My old pattern would have been to pile on initiatives. More priorities meant more opportunities to demonstrate value. If leadership was about solving problems, then more problems meant more leadership.

But I'd started to see the cost of this logic. Every additional priority diluted focus. Every new initiative competed for the same constrained resources. The organization was doing many things adequately instead of a few things exceptionally.

So, in the planning session, when we'd identified our top priorities, I did something radical: I published a **No List** alongside them.

YES List:

- Launch product v2.0 in Q2
- Reduce customer onboarding time from 10 days to 5
- Expand into two new markets

NO List:

- No new product features beyond v2.0 roadmap until launch
- No rebranding initiatives this year
- No new market exploration until current expansions stabilize
- No new partnerships until integration backlog is cleared

The No List was longer than the Yes list.

The reaction was mixed. Some leaders looked relieved, finally, permission to focus. Others looked frustrated, their pet projects had just been explicitly deprioritized.

One VP pushed back: "But what if an opportunity comes up that's too good to pass?"

"Then we explicitly decide what to drop from the Yes list," I said. "We don't pretend we can do everything. We choose."

That No List did something powerful. It gave teams language to push back on requests that came later. When someone proposed a new initiative midquarter, teams could point to the No List and say, "We made a deliberate choice to focus elsewhere. If this is truly urgent, what should we stop doing?"

Focus became defensible. Strategy became real.

Leaders don't just choose what to do—they defend what not to do.

Not Every Decision Deserves a Committee

One of my most uncomfortable leadership resets came when I looked at my calendar. It was full, but not with strategy, customers, or talent conversations. It was packed with approvals. Small decisions. Medium decisions. Decisions that could easily have been reversed if they went wrong. Yet everything seemed to find its way to my desk. At some point, I had to ask myself a harder question:
Was I adding value—or just adding latency?

That's when I noticed the real pattern. We weren't slow because people lacked capability. We were slow because we treated every decision as if it carried the same risk.

So we reset the rules.

If a decision could be undone without long-term damage, teams were expected to act quickly—without escalation. No performative alignment. No protective emails copied "just in case." If a decision had structural or irreversible consequences, we slowed it down and applied judgment deliberately.

The impact was immediate and slightly unsettling.

My calendar cleared. Decisions started happening without me. And nothing broke.

In fact, something else happened. The few decisions that truly required senior input became sharper—because they weren't buried under trivial ones. What surprised me most was this: speed didn't come from pushing people to decide faster. It came from making it safe to decide at all.

That was the reset.

Leading by Example: Making the Invisible Visible

The first shift was making my own reset visible to the team.

When I started protecting thinking time or stepped back from problems I would have historically solved, I did it publicly. Not to virtue signal—but to give permission.

In team meetings, I'd say things like: "I spent yesterday offline thinking about our Q3 strategy. That's why I wasn't responding to emails. The clarity I got was worth more than anything in my inbox."

When someone solved a problem without me, I'd celebrate it explicitly: "I love that you designed this solution without escalating. That's exactly the ownership we need more of."

When I published a No List for my own priorities, I shared it with the broader organization: "Here's what I'm saying no to this quarter so I can focus on what matters most. I encourage you to do the same."

These small acts of visibility shifted the culture from busyness-as-virtue to thoughtfulness-as-virtue.

The Meeting Reformation

One of the most impactful cultural changes was reforming our meeting structure: 45-minute defaults instead of hour-long blocks, walking 1-on-1s instead of conference rooms, and no-meeting Thursdays to protect thinking time.

The close-out script: Every decision-making meeting ended with a simple test: Can two people restate the decision in their own words? If not, we didn't have a decision yet, we had an illusion of agreement. This five-point close-out ritual prevented weeks of drift.

But at organizational scale, I added one critical element that made the difference between personal practice and cultural transformation: I made the new norms explicitly visible. The change went beyond my own calendar. I reset our team calendar defaults and asked my direct reports to take walking one-on-ones with their teams as well. The practices cascaded because they were modeled, named, and reinforced consistently.

Artifacts Over Adjectives

The most visible cultural shift was how we reported progress.

I banned status language like "on track," "progressing well," or color-coded dashboards. These invited theatre. Instead, every update was reduced to two lines:

- **Delivered (last 7 days):** Link to actual artifact—code deployed, document signed, test results published
- **Next (7 days):** Dated deliverable with clear definition of done

The first few weeks, the updates looked ugly. Gaps showed up everywhere. People were uncomfortable.

But something powerful happened: trust grew. Because reality was finally visible, we could address problems early instead of discovering them late. Teams stopped managing perception and started managing outcomes.

Progress stopped being a story on a slide and started being something you could click, test, and use.

Chapter 2
The Leadership Reset

The Reset Meeting Close-Out

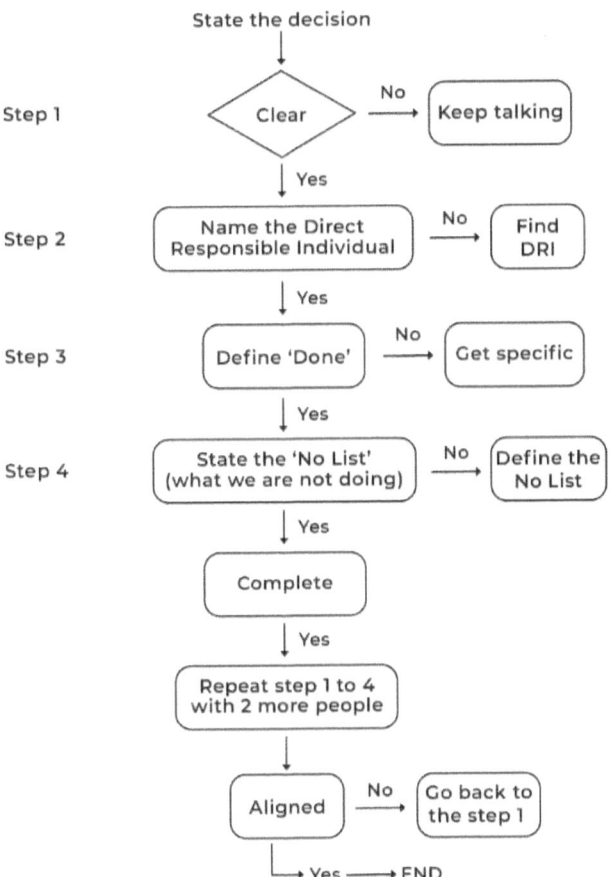

The 60-second meeting close that prevents weeks of confusion. If you can't pass this test, you don't have a decision yet. this can be at the bottom of the chart

The 60-second meeting close that prevents weeks of confusion. If you can't pass this test, you don't have a decision yet. This can be at the bottom of the chart.

When You're Not in Charge

Everything I've described assumes senior leadership authority. If you're a middle manager, the playbook is different but the principles hold.

The specific addition for this chapter: start where you have authority. You may not control company culture, but you control your team's culture. Implement the reset principles with your direct reports first. Model the behavior. Track the results. Success becomes its own permission.

The Path Forward

Two years into my reset, I barely recognize my old leadership patterns. I still work hard. I'm still demanding. I still hold high standards. But I'm no longer the hero of every story. I've become something more valuable: a builder of systems that work without me.

The shift wasn't dramatic. There was no single moment of transformation. It accumulated through dozens of small decisions:

- Stepping back when I wanted to jump in
- Naming an owner when I wanted to solve it myself
- Forcing clarity when consensus felt easier
- Publishing what I wasn't doing alongside what I was
- Celebrating team capability instead of personal heroics

The results speak for themselves. My team is more capable. Our delivery is more consistent. Problems get solved faster because they don't have to route through me. The organization is stronger, not because I'm working harder, but because I've stopped being the bottleneck.

But perhaps the most unexpected result: I'm more effective than I've ever been. Not despite doing less, but because of it.

When I stopped trying to solve every problem, I finally had time to think about which problems mattered. When I stopped chasing consensus, decisions moved faster and execution improved. When I stopped leaning on title and control, I discovered trust and clarity were far more powerful.

The leadership reset isn't about working less. It's about leading differently. It's about trading the addiction to heroics for the discipline of building capacity. It's about making the system the hero instead of yourself.

Actions for Readers: Your Reset Toolkit

If you recognize patterns of heroic leadership in yourself—if you're indispensable, if fires keep appearing that only you can put out, if your team waits for you to solve things, here's how to start your reset:

Start Small:

- Identify your hero pattern. What's the recurring crisis where you always jump in? Write it down. Now ask: "What would need to be true for this to get solved without me next time?"
- Choose one initiative or problem that you'd normally solve yourself. Name someone else as the Directly Responsible Individual(DRI). Give them clarity on the outcome and boundaries, then step back.

Build the Habit:

- Publish your No List. Write down 3-5 things you're explicitly not doing this quarter. Share it with your team. Give them permission to focus.
- Replace one status meeting with artifact reviews. Instead of asking "How's it going?" ask: "What shipped last week? Show me." Demand links to actual work, not summaries.

Go Deep:

- Block your first reset day. Schedule one full day in the next 90 days with no meetings, no email. Use it to think about: What problems keep recurring that only I can solve? What would need to be true for them to get solved without me? What capabilities does my team need that they're not building because I keep jumping in? Come back with at least one structural change to implement.
- Train your team on the reset framework. Share the shift from title/control/consensus to trust/clarity/ownership/speed with your direct reports. Make it explicit that you're changing how you lead and why. Invite them to hold you accountable when you slip back into hero mode.
- Measure the reset. Track one metric that shows whether you're building capacity or creating dependency: How many recurring problems are getting solved without your intervention? How many decisions are your directs making without escalating to you? How much time are you spending on strategic thinking vs. firefighting? Review quarterly. If the numbers aren't shifting, you're not actually resetting—you're just talking about it.

A Closing Story

Two years into my reset, we faced another urgent hiring crisis. Different client, same pressure. HR came to me: "Can you jump in like before?"

Every instinct from my old playbook urged me to say yes. But I'd learned: every time I jumped in, I prevented someone else from learning to jump.

So, I said: "No. But I'll help you build the capacity to handle this yourself."

Over two days, we defined the outcome (not "hire people" but "75 qualified candidates, 50 offers, six weeks"), named her as DRI with full authority, identified constraints, mapped resources, and set up weekly reviews.

Chapter 2
The Leadership Reset

Then I stepped back. It was uncomfortable. Progress seemed slow. I wanted to intervene.

But I held back. Six weeks later, they hit the target—not my way, but effectively.

The HR lead emailed after: "I won't lie, I wished you'd take over like before. But I'm glad you didn't. We learned more from struggling through this than from watching you fix it."

That's when I knew the reset had stuck. Leadership isn't whether you can solve every problem. It's whether you build systems and develop people so problems get solved without you.

The old me would have jumped in, saved the day, earned applause.

The new me built capacity that will last long after I'm gone.

That's the leadership reset: from being the hero to building heroes. From being indispensable to making yourself obsolete. From title, control, and consensus to trust, clarity, ownership, and speed.

It's harder. It's less immediately gratifying. It doesn't feed the ego the same way.

But it builds something far more valuable than a personal reputation: it builds organizations that can thrive without depending on any single person to save them.

In the next chapter, I'll show you how trust becomes the operating system that makes all of this possible. Because without trust, even the best systems fail.

And in the end, that's what real leadership looks like.

Chapter 3
Trust is the Operating System

"Empowered Teams are on the 3rd floor, Disruptive Technologies on the 7th, and Visionary Leadership on the 12th. For Trust, please raise a ticket."

The Impossible Goal

"You want me to do what?"

I was sitting across from my CFO, trying to process what he'd just asked. Build EY's global delivery center for finance services. From scratch. Scale it to become one of the world's largest finance delivery hubs. Oh, and do it on an aggressive timeline with limited precedent to follow.

I had never built anything remotely like this before. The scope was daunting. The operational complexity made my head spin. And the stakes were brutally clear: if this failed, I wouldn't just be managing a setback—I'd be the cautionary tale people whispered about in hallways.

Several colleagues had already warned me privately. "If this goes south, you're the one they'll blame," one said over coffee. "You sure you want to take this on?"

I wasn't sure. Not even close.

But as I sat in that meeting with my CFO, listening to him outline the vision, something else was happening beneath my uncertainty. I was calibrating a different question entirely: Do I trust him?

Not "Can I do this?" but "Will he back me when this gets hard?"

Because I knew it would get hard. Projects this ambitious always do. There would be moments when clients questioned our capabilities, when team members doubted the plan, when the pressure to deliver would be crushing. In those moments, would my CFO stand with me—or would he distance himself to protect his own position?

I watched him as he spoke. I'd worked with him for years. I'd seen how he handled crises. I'd watched him support leaders who took risks, even when those risks didn't pay off. I'd never seen him throw someone under the bus to save face.

That's when I realized: I trusted him completely.

Chapter 3
Trust is the Operating System

And that trust—more than any project plan, more than any budget allocation, more than any strategic framework—was what gave me the courage to say yes.

"I'll do it," I said. "But I'm going to need that same trust extended down through the organization. If we're going to pull this off, people are going to have to take risks without waiting for permission. They're going to have to tell hard truths when things aren't working. They're going to have to lean in when the safe move is to pull back."

He nodded. "That's exactly what I'm counting on."

Neither of us knew it then, but that conversation set the foundation for everything that followed. Not a technology strategy. Not an operational blueprint. Trust.

The Foundation I Didn't See

Three months into building the delivery center, I faced my first real test.

We'd landed a major client—a global financial services firm that would serve as our proof of concept. The engagement was complex: migrating their month-end close process to our center while maintaining quality standards and meeting aggressive timelines.

My team was talented but inexperienced with this level of complexity. I could see the nervousness in their faces during the kick-off meeting. They were waiting for me to tell them exactly how to execute, step by step.

My instinct was to do exactly that. I knew month-end close inside and out. I could have written the playbook, designed the workflow, prescribed every decision. It would have felt safe. It would have made me indispensable.

But something stopped me.

I remembered my CFO's trust in me—how he'd given me the goal and the boundaries but not the detailed playbook. How that trust had forced me to rise to the challenge rather than follow instructions. How it had made me feel capable rather than dependent.

So, in that kick-off meeting, I did something that felt deeply uncomfortable. I outlined the outcome we needed—flawless close within five business days, zero critical errors—and the constraints we had to respect. Then I said: "How we get there is yours to figure out. I trust you to design the approach. I'll support you, but I won't dictate the solution."

The silence that followed was painful.

Finally, one of the team leads spoke up: "What if we get it wrong?"

"Then we'll figure it out together," I said. "But I'd rather you own a solution that's 80% perfect than execute my solution at 100%. Because next time, I won't be in the room, and you'll need to know you can do this without me."

That statement hung in the air. I could see the mix of anxiety and something else—maybe excitement?—in their faces.

Over the next six weeks, I watched them struggle. There were moments when I wanted desperately to jump in, to course-correct, to impose my experience. But I held back. I asked questions instead of giving answers. I helped them think through problems rather than solving problems for them.

The first month-end close wasn't perfect. They missed the five-day target by half a day. But the process they'd designed was sound, and more importantly, it was theirs.

The second month, they hit the target.

Chapter 3
Trust is the Operating System

By the third month, they were improving the process without my input.

That's when I understood something fundamental: trust isn't just about believing in people—it's about giving them room to prove they're worthy of that belief.

Over the next two years, this pattern repeated: trust, delegate, step back. But I was about to learn that trust isn't something you build once—it's something you can break in a single moment.

The Moment I Broke Trust

Six months into the build, we hit a crisis.

A critical client deliverable was at risk. The team working on it had run into technical issues they couldn't resolve quickly. The client was growing impatient. The pressure from above was mounting.

And I panicked.

Instead of supporting the team through the problem, I took over. I jumped into the technical details, overrode their decisions, and personally drove the solution. We delivered on time, and the client was satisfied.

Mission accomplished, right?

Wrong.

A week later, one of my best team leads—someone I'd been grooming for bigger responsibilities—came to my office and closed the door.

"Can I be direct with you?" she asked.

"Always," I said.

Lead Less, Build More

"When you took over last week, it sent a message: that you don't actually trust us when things get hard. That all that talk about empowerment was fine for low-stakes work, but when it really mattered, you'd take the reins back."

The words hit like a punch.

"That's not—" I started to defend myself, but she cut me off gently.

"I know that's not what you meant. But it's what we heard. And now we're wondering: does he really trust us, or was that just nice words when things were easy?"

After she left, I sat in my office feeling gutted. Because she was right. I'd preached trust and empowerment, but the moment the stakes got high enough, I'd reverted to my old pattern: the heroic leader swooping in to save the day. I'd broken the very trust I'd worked months to build.

That night, I couldn't sleep. I kept replaying the conversation. And I realized something important: trust isn't a speech you give at a kick-off meeting—it's a promise you keep when keeping it is hardest.

The next morning, I called a team meeting. No agenda, no prepared remarks. Just honesty.

"I need to apologize," I said. "Last week, when we hit that crisis, I didn't trust you to handle it. I took over because I was scared—scared of failure, scared of letting the client down, scared of what it would mean for my reputation. And in doing that, I broke your trust."

The room was quiet.

"I can't promise I won't feel that fear again," I continued. "But I can promise that next time, I'll resist the urge to take over. I'll coach you through it instead of doing it for you. Because if I keep rescuing you, you'll never build the confidence to do this without me."

One of the team members spoke up: "What if we fail?"

"Then we'll fail together," I said. "And we'll learn from it together. But I'd rather fail while building your capability than succeed while undermining it."

I don't know if they fully believed me in that moment. Trust, once broken, isn't repaired with words. It's repaired with consistent behavior over time.

Over the next several months, I faced that same temptation again and again—to jump in, to take over, to be the hero. Each time, I forced myself to step back, to coach instead of solve, to trust instead of control.

It wasn't perfect. There were stumbles. But gradually, something shifted. The team stopped looking to me for answers and started trusting their own judgment. Problems got solved faster because they didn't wait for my approval. Innovation accelerated because people felt safe trying new approaches.

And our client relationships deepened, because the clients weren't just trusting me—they were trusting the entire team.

That crisis taught me that trust is built in ordinary moments but tested in critical ones. And if you fail the test, you have to earn it back—not through grand gestures, but through small, consistent acts that prove you've changed.

The Operating System I Couldn't See

It took me longer than it should have to understand what was actually happening as the delivery center grew.

On the surface, we were building processes, hiring people, implementing technology, and delivering client work. Those were the visible elements—the applications, if you will.

But underneath all of that, something more fundamental was emerging: an operating system built on trust.

I started noticing patterns. When we faced unexpected challenges, teams didn't freeze waiting for direction—they moved. When clients raised concerns, our people responded with transparency rather than defensiveness. When someone made a mistake, they reported it early instead of hiding it.

These weren't behaviors I'd mandated in any handbook. They weren't the result of policies or incentives. They emerged from an environment where people trusted that honesty wouldn't be punished, that risk-taking was supported, and that the organization had their back.

One day, a client asked me how we managed to execute so quickly compared to our competitors. I started to answer with our standard pitch about processes and talent, but then I stopped myself.

"Honestly?" I said. "It's trust. Our people don't wait for permission because they trust they won't be second-guessed. They tell us about problems early because they trust we'll help solve them, not blame them. They take intelligent risks because they trust we'll support them even if things don't work out perfectly."

The client looked skeptical. "Trust is great, but surely there's more to it than that?"

"There is," I said. "We have good processes, talented people, solid technology. But here's what I've learned: all those things are like apps on a phone. If the operating system is corrupted, even the best apps won't run properly. Trust is our operating system. Everything else runs on top of it."

That conversation crystallized something I'd been sensing but hadn't articulated: organizations that treat trust as a "soft" nice-to-have are missing the point entirely.

Trust isn't decoration.

It's infrastructure.

The Equation I Had to Learn

My understanding of trust evolved gradually, shaped by both successes and failures. Eventually, I came across a framework that helped me make sense of what I'd been learning through experience: the Trust Equation.

$$Trust = (Credibility + Reliability + Intimacy) \div Self\text{-}Orientation$$

When I first encountered this formula from David Maister and colleagues, it felt academic. But as I mapped it against my own experiences, it became powerfully practical.

Credibility: The Foundation That Wasn't Enough

Early in my career, I'd assumed credibility was everything. If I was the smartest person in the room, if I had the right answers, if my expertise was unquestionable—surely that would generate trust?

It didn't.

I learned this during my first major client presentation. I'd prepared meticulously, knew every data point, anticipated every question. My technical knowledge was impeccable.

But the client didn't trust me. And I couldn't figure out why.

A mentor pulled me aside afterward: "You were credible," he said. "But credibility alone doesn't create trust. They need to know you're credible about things that matter to them, not just credible in general."

That feedback changed how I thought about credibility. It's not about demonstrating everything you know—it's about demonstrating clarity on what the other person needs to know.

I watched a junior analyst do this beautifully in a later meeting. She was explaining a complex SAP report to senior executives. Instead of showcasing her technical depth, she translated the complexity into three simple insights that mattered for the decision at hand. Her credibility came from clarity, not comprehensiveness.

Credibility, I learned, is about congruence between what you say and what you stand for. Warren Buffett's annual letters work not because they're full of financial jargon, but because his candid, plain-spoken style matches his long-standing values. When Patagonia ran ads telling people "Don't Buy This Jacket" to promote environmental consciousness, it deepened their credibility because it aligned perfectly with their established identity.

Credibility comes not from expertise alone, but from authentic expertise that is clearly expressed and consistently demonstrated.

Reliability: The Discipline I Undervalued

If Credibility was knowing the right things. Reliability was doing the right things, every time it mattered.

I used to think reliability meant big heroic acts. But I learned it's built in small, unsexy disciplines.

One practice transformed my leadership: I stopped canceling one-on-ones.

In my early years, I'd regularly cancel when "something more important" came up. Each cancellation sent an unintended message: "You're not actually a priority."

So, I implemented a rule: one-on-ones happen unless I'm hospitalized. Client crisis? We keep the one-on-one and I might need to cut it short, but we start it. Executive meeting conflict? I reschedule the executive meeting. Urgent fire? We meet, and I might need their help thinking through the fire.

The change was small. The impact was profound.

Over months, I noticed people bringing harder conversations to me earlier. They'd surface problems when they were still small rather than waiting until they became crises. They'd share concerns about their career development, team dynamics, or strategic direction—things they'd been holding back.

When I asked one team member why she felt comfortable raising difficult topics now, she said: "Because you show up. Every week, no matter what. It tells me I matter, which makes me trust that you'll actually listen to what I say."

Reliability, I learned, is the compound interest of trust. Small deposits made consistently create large reserves over time.

Intimacy: The Safety I Had to Create

Intimacy in the Trust Equation doesn't mean friendship or personal closeness. It means psychological safety—the confidence that you won't be punished, humiliated, or marginalized for speaking up, asking questions, or admitting mistakes.

I learned about intimacy's importance through its absence.

In one of our early client engagements, we were running weekly status meetings. On paper, everything looked fine—green dashboards, positive updates, confident presentations. But I started noticing something odd: our actual delivery kept hitting unexpected snags that should have been visible earlier.

One evening, I cornered one of the team leads privately: "Why am I learning about these issues days after they emerge? What's happening in the status meetings?"

She hesitated, then said: "People don't feel safe raising problems. In the first few meetings, when someone mentioned a risk, they got grilled—'Why didn't you prevent this?' 'Who's responsible?' 'What's your plan to fix it?' It felt like punishment, not problem-solving. So now people just... don't mention things until they're too big to hide."

I was stunned. I thought I was being rigorous, holding people accountable. They experienced it as creating an environment where honesty was dangerous.

I changed our approach immediately. In the next status meeting, I opened with: "I've realized we're not creating space for hard truths. From now on, this meeting's purpose is transparency, not judgment. If you flag a risk early, my first response will be 'Thank you for raising that—how can we help?' not 'Why did this happen?'"

The first meeting after that statement was still cautious. But someone did raise a small risk. I kept my word: "Thanks for surfacing that. What support do you need?"

By the third week, the dynamic had transformed. Problems surfaced early. People asked for help before situations became critical. Our delivery improved because we were dealing with reality instead of managed perception.

Amy Edmondson's research on psychological safety makes this point powerfully: teams where people feel safe admitting mistakes and voicing concerns consistently outperform teams where brilliance is high but safety is low. Google's Project Aristotle confirmed this—psychological safety was the single strongest predictor of team effectiveness.

Intimacy is about creating an environment where people trust that honesty won't be weaponized against them.

Self-Orientation: The Poison I Had to Confront

The denominator in the Trust Equation is self-orientation—and it's a divider for good reason. Even high credibility, reliability, and intimacy collapse if people sense your primary motivation is only yourself.

I confronted this during a client pitch. The opportunity was significant—for the client and for my career. Winning this would position me for promotion.

During the pitch, I emphasized aspects that would make me look good rather than what would actually serve the client best. I proposed a more complex engagement than they needed because bigger meant more visible.

The client didn't bite. They chose a simpler approach from a competitor.

Afterward, my boss asked me to debrief. I blamed their pricing, risk aversion, timing.

He let me finish, then said quietly: "Or maybe they sensed you were selling what you needed, not what they needed."

The words stung because they were true.

I'd let self-orientation corrupt the pitch. Instead of diagnosing their actual need and proposing the right-sized solution, I'd designed a solution that served my ambitions. And clients have keen radar for that misalignment.

Herb Kelleher, Southwest Airlines' legendary CEO, demonstrated the opposite. When journalists wanted to praise him for the company's success, he consistently redirected credit to employees, to the culture, to the team. That outward orientation—visible and consistent—built trust not just in him but in the entire organization.

Self-orientation is trust's silent killer. People forgive mistakes in execution, but they don't forgive sensing that you're using them for your own ends.

The Trust Equation in Action

The most painful lesson in my leadership journey came when I watched trust collapse—not in a competitor's story or a business school case study, but in a project I was leading.

We'd taken on an ambitious ERP implementation for a client. The timeline was aggressive, but we'd committed to it. Six months in, we were behind schedule. Not catastrophically, but enough that the original deadline was clearly unrealistic.

I had two choices: tell the client early and reset expectations, or push the team harder and hope we could make up time.

I chose hope.

For the next two months, I drove the team relentlessly. We worked weekends. We cut corners on testing. We painted optimistic pictures in status meetings while privately worrying about quality. I told myself we were being resilient, pushing through adversity.

Chapter 3
Trust is the Operating System

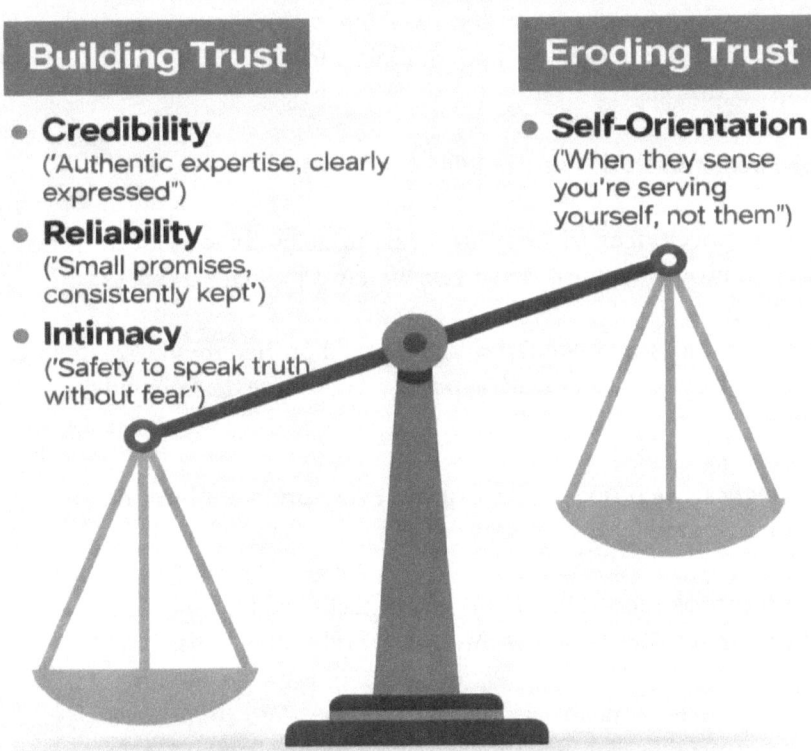

Trust = (Credibility + Reliability + Intimacy) / Self-Orientation.

Even high credibility and reliability collapses if self interest develops

The scale tips based on the balance between these forces

We hit the deadline. Barely. The system went live.

And within two weeks, it started breaking. Critical processes failed. Data integrity issues emerged. Users couldn't complete basic workflows. The client was furious.

The system survived. Trust didn't

The client no longer trusted our status updates. If we'd been misleading them about our readiness, what else were we hiding?

The team no longer trusted my judgment. I'd pushed them to deliver something we all knew wasn't ready, and now they were dealing with the consequences.

I no longer trusted myself. I'd violated every principle I claimed to believe about transparency and honesty.

The repair took months. Not months of technical fixes—we resolved most of the system issues in weeks. Months of rebuilding trust.

With the client, it meant radical transparency. We shared every issue immediately, no matter how embarrassing. We published our entire backlog of defects. We gave them direct access to our project management tools. It felt vulnerable and uncomfortable. But slowly, issue by issue, their confidence began to return.

With the team, it meant acknowledging I'd failed them. Not just in a vague "sorry things got hard" way, but specifically: "I knew we weren't ready. I pushed you to go live anyway because I was scared of having a difficult conversation with the client. I broke your trust by prioritizing my own discomfort over your professional judgment. I won't make that mistake again."

One team member told me later: "The apology mattered, but what mattered more was that you actually changed. The next time we hit a crunch, you didn't push us to cut corners—you helped us have the hard conversation with the client about what was realistic."

Trust, once broken, can be repaired. But repair requires three things:

Acknowledge the breach plainly. No euphemisms, no blame-shifting. Name what happened and own your role in it.

Apologize without conditions. "I'm sorry if you felt..." is not an apology. "I'm sorry I did X, which caused Y" is.

Act differently, consistently. Words repair nothing. Only changed behavior over time rebuilds trust.

This pattern isn't unique to me. Johnson & Johnson's handling of the 1982 Tylenol crisis remains the gold standard: they acknowledged the danger immediately, recalled 31 million bottles at enormous cost, and redesigned packaging to prevent tampering. Trust, initially shattered, returned stronger than before.

Contrast that with the corporate half-apologies we see regularly: "We're sorry if anyone was offended..." These make things worse because they signal you don't actually understand what you did wrong.

Trust breaks when we prioritize comfort over honesty. It repairs when we do the opposite.

The Asymmetry Nobody Talks About

One insight about trust changed how I thought about leadership responsibility: *trust flows asymmetrically through power structures.*

When I, as a senior leader, said "I trust you" to a team member, it cost me relatively little. If they failed, I had organizational buffers, other opportunities, financial reserves. My career might take a hit, but I'd survive.

When a team member trusted me, they were betting their livelihood, their reputation, and sometimes their family's financial security. Any failure on my part carried a cost to them that far exceeded the cost to me

This asymmetry creates a fundamental ethical obligation: leaders must guard others' trust more carefully than their own interests.

I learned this watching employees navigate a reorganization. Senior executives debated options over months, exploring various scenarios. For them, each option was manageable—they'd land somewhere solid regardless.

For individual contributors and middle managers, each option represented profound uncertainty. Would their role exist? Would they need to relocate? Would their manager change? The anxiety was palpable while leaders casually discussed "options."

When I finally understood this dynamic, it changed how I communicated during uncertainty. Instead of presenting options as if we were all equally exposed, I began to acknowledge the asymmetry. I would say, 'I know this uncertainty is harder on you than on me. Here's everything I know, here's what I don't know yet, and here's when I expect to have more clarity.' Leaders like Satya Nadella have practiced this openly during periods of transformation, and I saw it modeled credibly by Mike Ventling during his time as CFO at EY. Naming uncertainty without hiding behind false reassurance didn't weaken trust. It strengthened it.

That simple acknowledgment didn't eliminate their anxiety, but it honored the reality of their position. And honoring reality is a foundational element of trust.

Chapter 3
Trust is the Operating System

Building Trust at Scale

Individual trust is one thing. Building it across an organization of hundreds or thousands is different.

As the delivery center grew, I couldn't personally build trust with every person. I needed trust to scale systematically.

The shift from personal practice to organizational design required three trust-specific moves:

Trust through autonomy: Eliminated approval layers for decisions under defined thresholds. Teams could act without permission if they could explain their reasoning.

Trust through vulnerability: Published failures monthly in "lessons learned" forums. Leadership shared their mistakes first. This normalized honesty over performance.

Trust through transparency: Shared client feedback, financial results, and strategic challenges widely—even when uncomfortable. Reality builds credibility faster than managed messaging.

These weren't my innovations alone—they emerged from watching organizations that had cracked the code on trust at scale.

Netflix's famous "freedom and responsibility" culture eliminated vacation policies and expense approvals, trusting employees to act like adults. The result wasn't chaos but heightened accountability.

Nordstrom's famous one-rule employee handbook demonstrates this trust principle perfectly: "Use good judgment in all situations." That's it. No elaborate policies, no approval matrices. Just trust that employees understand the goal—exceptional customer service—and will make good decisions.

Patagonia tells employees to surf when the waves are good. This sounds frivolous until you understand the logic: trusting people to manage their own time and energy produces more engaged, creative work than rigid scheduling ever could.

The pattern across these organizations: they designed systems that demonstrated trust, not just talked about it.

The Trust I Left Behind

Five years after that initial conversation with my CFO, I was preparing to transition to a new role. The delivery center had grown beyond anything we'd imagined that first day, thousands of people, dozens of clients, global reach.

In my final all-hands meeting, someone asked me what I was most proud of.

I almost gave the standard answer: the scale we'd achieved, the client relationships we'd built, the financial results we'd delivered.

But that wasn't the truth.

"I'm most proud," I said, "that we built an organization where people ask 'have we built enough trust to try?' before launching bold initiatives. That question, whether we have sufficient trust, is now part of how you evaluate readiness. That's the legacy that matters."

Because here's what I'd learned through all those years: strategies change, technologies evolve, processes get redesigned. But if the operating system of trust is healthy, the organization adapts. If it's not, even the best strategies fail.

A few months after I left, the center faced a major crisis, a client threatened to pull a large contract over quality concerns. I wasn't there to manage it.

Chapter 3
Trust is the Operating System

The team handled it brilliantly. They acknowledged the issues without defensiveness, shared their corrective action plan transparently, and invited the client into the solution. The contract not only stayed—it expanded.

When I heard about it, I felt something unexpected: relief.

Not because they'd saved the contract, but because they'd done it without me. The trust I'd worked to build wasn't dependent on my presence. It had become embedded in how they operated.

You know trust has become truly systemic when it continues to hold even without you.

Building Your Trust Operating System

Trust isn't built through grand gestures, it's built through small, consistent practices that accumulate over time. Here's how to start:

The Foundation (Start Today):

Close your say-do gap. List the last three commitments you made to your team. Were they all kept? If not, repair one immediately—not with excuses, but with acknowledgement and action.

Practice the 2x1 ratio. In your next three meetings, for every statement you make, ask two questions and listen twice as long. This builds intimacy and reduces self-orientation simultaneously.

Test your self-orientation. Before your next major decision or recommendation, ask: "Am I proposing what's best for them, or what's best for my career?" If you sense misalignment, reset.

The Practice (This Month):

Never cancel one-on-ones. Block recurring time with each direct report. Protect it like you'd protect a meeting with your CEO. Show up consistently, and watch what people feel safe sharing.

Share one uncomfortable truth. In your next team meeting, share something you're worried about or uncertain of. Model that acknowledging weakness builds trust faster than projecting invincibility.

Implement the failure-sharing ritual. Start a monthly "what we learned" forum where people share mistakes and lessons. Leadership goes first. Normalize truth-telling as strength, not risk.

The System (This Quarter):

Eliminate one approval layer. Find a decision category where you're the bottleneck. Define clear boundaries and decision criteria, then push authority down. Track what happens—you'll likely find speed increases while quality stays high.

Create your trust dashboard. Beyond financial and operational metrics, start tracking:

- Psychological safety scores (anonymous surveys)
- Decision cycle times for standard decisions
- How often problems are surfaced early vs. discovered late

Make trust as measurable as revenue.

Conduct a trust audit. Use the Trust Equation as your framework. Ask three people you trust to give you honest feedback:

- Credibility: Do my words match my actions? Am I clear or confusing?

- Reliability: Do I keep commitments, especially small ones?
- Intimacy: Do people feel safe being honest with me?
- Self-Orientation: Do I put the team's success ahead of my own visibility?

Listen without defending. Then act on what you hear.

Long-Term: Make Trust Your Leadership Compass

Define your trust principles. Write down your personal leadership values, your non-negotiables. Post them visibly. Revisit them weekly. Let your team hold you accountable to them.

Repair something you've broken. Identify one relationship where trust has frayed—maybe through neglect, maybe through a specific breach. Acknowledge it, apologize genuinely, and commit to consistent different behavior. Then follow through.

Leave trust behind. The ultimate measure isn't whether people trust you while you're there, it's whether the trust you built persists after you leave. Ask yourself: "If I left tomorrow, would this team still operate with high trust? Or have I made trust dependent on me?"

If the answer is uncomfortable, start designing systems that embed trust beyond your personal presence.

A Final Reflection

When I started my leadership journey, I thought trust was about being liked, about being nice, about avoiding conflict.

I was wrong on all counts.

Lead Less, Build More

Trust is about being credible when you'd rather be comfortable, reliable when you'd rather be flexible, creating intimacy when you'd rather keep distance, and suppressing self-orientation when you'd rather claim credit.

Trust is hard. It's uncomfortable. It requires consistency when you're exhausted, honesty when you'd prefer spin, and humility when your ego wants validation.

But trust is also the only sustainable foundation for leadership that matters. Because you can't force people to follow you into uncertainty. You can't command people to take intelligent risks. You can't mandate people to tell you hard truths.

They'll only do those things if they trust you.

That kind of trust makes it possible to attempt things that would otherwise paralyze organizations driven by fear, politics, or control.

That's the question Tony Hsieh was really asking at Zappos when he attempted radical organizational experiments: "Have we built enough trust to try?"

It's the question my CFO was asking when he gave me the impossible goal of building a global delivery center.

And it's the question you need to ask before attempting anything bold: Have you built enough trust?

If the answer is yes, amazing things become possible.

If the answer is no, start building. Because trust is the operating system everything else runs on.

Upgrade it every day.

Chapter 3
Trust is the Operating System

I would like to end this chapter by pointing out that trust shows up differently at different levels of an organization, even though it is built from the same fundamentals. With individuals, trust is personal and experiential, shaped by reliability, fairness, and how leaders behave when risk is uneven. Within a team, trust becomes behavioral, reinforced through shared norms, clear decision rights, and consistent follow-through. Across a team of teams, trust turns systemic, carried less by personal relationships and more by context, transparency, and well-designed interfaces. At that scale, trust no longer depends on who is present in the room. It holds because the system itself makes trustworthy behavior the default.

Chapter 4
Hierarchy Doesn't Guarantee Results

Stairway to (Empowerment) Heaven?

The Question Nobody Asked

The Finance Executive Committee meeting in Jersey City was exactly what you'd expect: floor-to-ceiling windows overlooking the Hudson, leather chairs, polished mahogany. I was the only non-CFO invited—a signal my work was being noticed.

The global CFO presented an ambitious restructuring: new roles, redrawn reporting lines, complex org charts with matrix relationships. Around the table, regional CFOs nodded approval. "Makes sense." "Good thinking."

But something bothered me. The interplay between the new "Area Finance Leader" role and existing functional heads seemed ambiguous. Who would have final say when priorities conflicted?

My pulse quickened. The rational part of my brain calculated risk: You're just a guest here. These are seasoned CFOs with decades more experience. Asking a basic question might make you look naive. Or worse, arrogant, as if you think you understand their business better than they do.

But another voice was getting louder: If you're confused, others probably are too. And if this ambiguity exists now, it will become chaos in execution.

The CFO was moving to the next slide. The moment to speak was passing.

I raised my hand.

The room went quiet. Several pairs of eyes turned toward me—some curious, some surprised that the guest was interrupting the flow.

"How exactly do you see the AFL role interplaying with the functional head role?" I asked. "When there's a conflict in priorities or resource allocation, who has the final call?"

The CFO stopped. For a moment, he looked taken aback. Then he slowly set down his presentation remote.

"That's a good question," he said quietly. "Honestly, I don't have a clear answer yet. Let me reflect on it and come back to the group."

Chapter 4
Hierarchy Doesn't Guarantee Results

The tension in the room shifted. A few CFOs glanced at each other. One person jotted a note. The meeting continued, but something had changed.

Afterward, as I was washing my hands in the restroom, one of the regional CFOs approached me.

"I'm glad you asked that," he said, keeping his voice low even though we were alone. "It needed to be said. Frankly, I should have said it myself."

I nodded, still processing what had happened. "Why didn't you?"

He smiled ruefully. "Because I have a title to protect. You had the freedom to ask what we were all thinking."

That conversation stayed with me for years. Because it revealed something fundamental about hierarchy that I'd been slow to understand: the org chart doesn't show who has influence—it shows who has permission to speak.

And sometimes, the person without the title is the only one free enough to tell the truth.

Authority I Thought I Had

My first real leadership role came in the mid-1990s: finance head at an engineering firm. Young, ambitious, convinced the title would do the heavy lifting.

The hiring had been rigorous, and I had beaten more experienced candidates. On my first day, the CEO walked me through strategy, stakeholders, responsibilities. I left energized, ready to make my mark.

As I stood to leave, he paused and looked at me directly.

"Sooner or later," he said quietly, "you'll realize you're responsible for things you never imagined you would be responsible for."

The words stopped me. "Isn't my role clearly defined?" I asked, confused.

He smiled gently. "Yes. Your role is very clearly defined." Then he waved goodbye and said nothing more.

For days, those words troubled me. At the time, I didn't understand what he meant. How could I be held accountable for things outside my defined responsibilities? Wasn't the entire point of an org chart to make clear where my role ended and someone else's began?

I tried to shake it off. I had a job description. I had a title. I had clear reporting lines. Surely that was enough.

It wasn't.

Three months in, our month-end close process was broken, consistently late, error-prone, causing friction with business units. Technically, not my problem. The close process reported through a different part of finance, outside my scope.

But the business units didn't care about org charts. They cared that finance, which included me, wasn't delivering. They. And the dysfunction was affecting my team's work.

I had a choice: point to the org chart and say "not my responsibility," or step into the gap.

I stepped in. I pulled together the people who owned various pieces of the close, facilitated a redesign, worked with peers to implement it. Weeks of work that had nothing to do with my official job description.

When it was done, the CEO called me into his office.

Chapter 4
Hierarchy Doesn't Guarantee Results

"I heard you fixed the close process," he said.

"It needed fixing," I replied.

"It wasn't your responsibility."

"No," I agreed. "But it was affecting results. And results are everyone's responsibility."

He leaned back, and I saw that gentle smile again. "Now you understand what I meant on your first day."

> *That's when it clicked. The org chart defines your minimum accountability, what you'll be fired for not doing. But leadership is defined by what you choose to own beyond that minimum.*

I'd thought my title would give me authority. What I learned was that authority comes from taking responsibility for things that matter, whether or not they're written in your job description.

When Hierarchy Became the Enemy

Five years into that role, I'd gotten comfortable. I understood how the organization worked, where the informal power resided, when to push and when to wait. I'd learned to work the system.

Then the company hired a new CEO as the former CEO retired.

He came from a much larger, more hierarchical organization. His instinct when facing any challenge was to clarify reporting lines, add approval layers, and tighten control. Within six months, he'd reorganized us three times, each iteration adding more structure, more defined roles, more formal processes.

On paper, it looked more professional. The org chart was cleaner. Roles were crisper. Approval chains were explicit.

In practice, everything slowed down.

Decisions that used to take days now took weeks as they routed through new approval layers. Problems we'd previously solved informally now required formal escalation. People who used to collaborate across boundaries now waited for permission to engage.

I watched a talented project manager, someone who had been instrumental in several successful initiatives, become paralyzed by the new structure.

She'd been empowered to make decisions, pull in resources as needed, and move fast. Now, every decision required three levels of approval. Every resource request went through a formal allocation process. Every problem required a steering committee meeting.

Within a year, she left. "I didn't sign up to navigate bureaucracy," she told me in her exit interview. "I signed up to solve problems. This place used to value initiative. Now it values following process."

She wasn't alone. Over eighteen months, we lost a third of our highest performers. Not to competitors offering more money—to companies offering more autonomy.

The CEO couldn't understand it. "We've created clarity," he insisted. "Everyone knows exactly who's responsible for what. How is that not better?"

But clarity about hierarchy isn't the same as clarity about results. The new structure had made authority clear while making actual work harder. We'd optimized for organizational neatness at the expense of organizational effectiveness.

The Townhall That Revealed Everything

The breaking point came during a virtual townhall. Hundreds logged in early, eager to hear the CEO address growing concerns about direction.

The start time passed. Five minutes. Then ten.

A board member appeared on screen: "The CEO has been delayed and cannot join. We'll reschedule. Thank you."

The Screen went black.

I sat there stunned, along with hundreds of others. We'd all cleared our calendars. The CEO had known about this for weeks. And in the moment when leadership needed to show up most, we got... nothing.

But what troubled me more than the cancellation was what happened next, or rather, what didn't happen

The board member who'd delivered the cancellation was perfectly positioned to step in. He was deeply involved in strategy. He knew what needed to be communicated. He'd been in all the planning sessions.

But he didn't even try. The assumption, his and apparently everyone else's, was that without the CEO there was nothing to say. Authority was so concentrated in one person that his absence meant organizational silence.

I thought about all the smart, capable leaders scattered across that cancelled call. Any one of them could have provided an update, addressed concerns, kept momentum going. But the hierarchy was so rigid that initiative had been trained out of the system.

That evening, I got a message from a colleague: "Did you notice who didn't show up for the townhall? The CEO. Did you notice who else didn't speak up? Everyone else. That tells you everything about where we are as an organization."

He was right. The org chart had become so dominant that people had forgotten they had voices independent of their boxes.

When hierarchy becomes the only source of authority, its absence doesn't create space for others to lead, it creates a vacuum where nothing happens.

The Pattern I Couldn't Unsee

Once I started noticing the dysfunction, I saw it everywhere.

In client work, I watched a transformation initiative stall because the designated leader had the title but not the trust. He'd been appointed to lead the change because his position on the org chart made sense, not because he'd earned credibility with the people who needed to execute it.

The result was predictable: teams nodded in meetings, then did nothing afterward. They weren't defying him overtly—that would have been insubordination. They were simply waiting for real leadership to emerge, and when it didn't, work ground to a halt.

I pulled him aside after one particularly tense steering committee meeting. "Do you know why this isn't working?" I asked.

He looked exhausted. "I've done everything by the book. I've followed the change management framework. I've engaged the stakeholders. What am I missing?"

"They don't trust you," I said. "And your title can't make them trust you."

Chapter 4
Hierarchy Doesn't Guarantee Results

"But I'm the designated transformation lead," he protested. "They have to follow the plan."

"They have to attend your meetings," I corrected. "They don't have to believe in you. And without that belief, compliance is the best you'll get. You need commitment."

He didn't want to hear it. Six months later, the transformation was quietly shelved, a victim of what the executive summary called "insufficient organizational readiness." But the real problem was simpler: hierarchy had appointed a leader, but the organization hadn't chosen to follow him.

Around the same time, I consulted with a technology startup scaling fast. They'd grown from 50 to 400 people in eighteen months, and the founders were grappling with structure.

"We need more hierarchy," one founder insisted. "It's chaos. No one knows who makes decisions. We need clear reporting lines."

But when I observed how they actually worked, I saw something different. Yes, it looked chaotic on paper. But problems got solved remarkably fast. Why? Because people didn't wait for organizational permission to act. If you saw a problem, you grabbed whoever had relevant expertise and fixed it.

One afternoon, I watched a junior engineer notice a potential security vulnerability. Instead of reporting up through channels, she pulled together a senior developer, a product manager, and someone from ops. Within two hours, they'd assessed the risk, designed a fix, and implemented it.

"That would never happen in a traditional hierarchy," I told the founder. "By the time that issue reached someone with authority to convene that group, the vulnerability would have been exploited."

"But we can't scale chaos," he argued.

"It's not chaos," I said. "It's distributed authority. People take ownership because they're empowered to act, not because they're told to."

The contrast was stark. The established company with clear hierarchy: slow, risk-averse, dependent on designated leaders. The startup with minimal hierarchy: fast, action-oriented, leadership emerging organically based on context and competence.

Hierarchy, I realized, optimizes for clarity of authority. But what organizations actually need is clarity of purpose and distributed ownership.

Authority vs. Influence

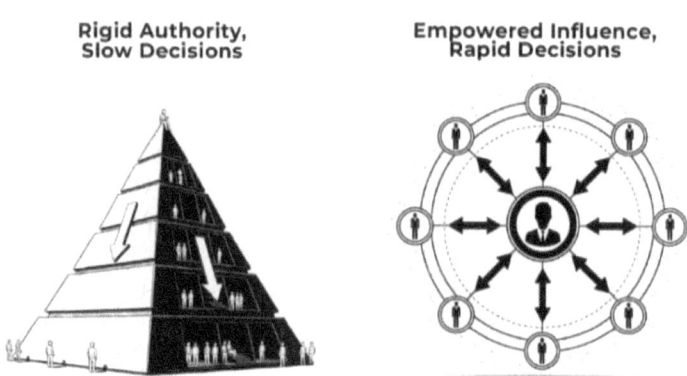

Learning from the Extremes

My understanding deepened when I studied organizations that had experimented with eliminating hierarchy entirely.

Ricardo Semler's transformation of Semco in Brazil became something of an obsession for me. In the early 1980s, Semler inherited a traditional

Chapter 4
Hierarchy Doesn't Guarantee Results

manufacturing company with rigid hierarchy, layers of management, fixed roles, bureaucratic processes.

He did something radical: he dismantled it all. Eliminated job titles. Let employees set their own schedules and salaries. Pushed strategic decisions down to those closest to the work.

Critics predicted chaos. Investors worried about accountability. Traditional management thinkers wrote him off as reckless.

Instead, Semco thrived. Productivity increased. Innovation accelerated. Profits grew. The company became a case study in how distributed authority could work at scale.

What fascinated me wasn't just that it worked, it was why it worked. Semler hadn't created anarchy. He'd created clarity of a different kind: clarity about purpose, principles, and boundaries. Instead of telling people how to work, he was clear about why the work mattered and what success looked like, then trusted people to figure out the how.

When a visiting executive asked Semler how decisions got made without hierarchy, Semler gestured to a group of employees intensely debating a production problem: "Decisions are made by those who step up, not by those who are told to."

But I also studied the failures. Zappos' attempt at Holacracy was particularly instructive. They eliminated traditional hierarchies entirely, replacing them with self-organizing circles and distributed authority.

It didn't work. Or more precisely, it worked for some parts of the organization but failed for others. Roles blurred. Accountability evaporated. Decision-making became exhausting as everything required consensus. About 18% of the workforce left rather than adapt to the new structure.

The lesson wasn't that flat structures don't work, it was that eliminating hierarchy requires replacing it with something equally clear. Zappos had removed structure without adequately defining what would replace it. Semco had removed hierarchy but maintained clarity about purpose, principles, and decision rights.

Netflix found a middle path: they kept formal hierarchy for structure and career paths, but decoupled it from decision-making authority. As Reed Hastings said: "We're a team, not a family. On a team, you're judged by performance, not position." Context and expertise trumped hierarchy.

The pattern across all these experiments became clear: successful organizations use structure to create clarity, not control. Failed experiments use structure to consolidate authority.

When Influence Replaces Authority

The transformation in my own thinking came gradually, shaped by these observations and my own experiments in leadership.

I started testing what happened when I deliberately didn't use my title as a source of authority. In meetings, I'd hold back from speaking first, even when I had strong opinions. I'd ask questions instead of giving answers. I'd look for opportunities to defer to others who had better context, even if I outranked them.

The results surprised me. At first, people looked uncertain, asking themselves why Suresh wasn't taking the lead? But once they realized I genuinely wanted their input, the quality of discussion improved dramatically. People brought ideas they'd been holding back. Debates became more substantive. Solutions emerged that I wouldn't have thought of on my own.

One practice became particularly powerful: "walking the floor." Instead of summoning people to my office, I'd go to theirs. Instead of formal

Chapter 4
Hierarchy Doesn't Guarantee Results

meetings, I'd have corridor conversations. Instead of asking for status updates, I'd ask: "What's working? What's broken? What do you need?"

These informal interactions gave me insight that no status report could provide. I learned about problems early, when they were still solvable. I heard ideas from people who wouldn't speak up in formal meetings. I built relationships based on genuine curiosity rather than hierarchical obligation.

A junior analyst once told me: "I thought you asking me questions was a test, like you already knew the answer and wanted to see if I did too. It took me months to realize you actually wanted my opinion."

That comment unsettled me because it revealed how thoroughly hierarchy had trained people to distrust curiosity from leaders. A senior person asking questions must be testing you, not learning from you. Authority was assumed to flow one direction.

But the most important shift came when I started explicitly giving away authority I didn't need to hoard.

During one strategic planning cycle, instead of presenting the plan I'd developed, I asked three team leads to develop proposals independently, then present them to the broader group. My role was to synthesize, not dictate.

One of my peers pulled me aside: "Why are you outsourcing strategy to your team? Isn't that your job?"

"My job is to get the best strategy," I said. "That doesn't mean I need to be the one who creates it."

The proposals that emerged were better than anything I would have developed alone. More importantly, the execution was faster and more committed because the people implementing the strategy had designed it.

That's when I understood: authority is about position, but influence is about impact. And impact comes from enabling others, not controlling them.

The Test of Absence

I learned that the ultimate test of leadership isn't what happens when you're in the room, it's what happens when you're not. If your absence creates paralysis, you haven't built leadership; you've built dependency. If your absence barely registers because the team keeps moving, you've done your job.

This principle applies doubly to hierarchy: formal authority that depends on your presence is fragile. Influence that persists in your absence is sustainable.

Building Authority That Scales

Once I understood this principle, I started deliberately designing for it. Not just in my own practice, but in how I shaped the broader organization.

We eliminated approval layers for decisions under certain thresholds. If someone could articulate their reasoning and the decision was reversible, they had authority to act. This shifted hundreds of small decisions from waiting for permission to rapid execution.

We made decision rights explicit by clarifying who provided input, who could veto, and who ultimately decided. More often than not, that person wasn't the most senior, but the one closest to the context

We publicly celebrated decisions that didn't come to me. When someone solved a problem without escalating it upward, I called it out. Over time, this shifted the norm from deferring decisions to taking ownership.

We made "stepping up" a valued behavior, not insubordination. If someone saw a gap and filled it without being asked, that was leadership, regardless of their title.

The cultural shift was gradual but unmistakable. In year one, people still looked to me for permission. By year three, they looked to me for coaching, but they made their own calls.

The data supported the transformation. Decision cycle times dropped by 40%. Employee engagement scores rose. Client satisfaction improved because problems were solved faster. And perhaps most telling: when I eventually moved to a different role, the organization's performance didn't drop—it continued improving.

That's when I knew we'd built something sustainable. Authority that scales isn't concentrated in a few people; it's distributed across everyone who has earned the right to exercise it.

One of my CFOs once told me that we should think of ourselves as a factory of CFOs. Our job wasn't just to run finance, but to develop people so well that they could evolve within the organization or succeed somewhere else. At first, that sounded risky. Over time, I realized it was the opposite. When leaders build systems that create capability rather than dependence, hierarchy stops being about control and starts being about multiplication."

When Hierarchy Actually Helps

But I'd be dishonest if I claimed hierarchy never serves a purpose. Through all my experimentation, I learned that the question isn't whether to have structure, it's what kind of structure serves your actual needs.

Accountability needs to be crystal clear. In regulated environments or high-risk situations, you need someone clearly accountable for outcomes.

Distributed authority can blur responsibility in ways that create legal or ethical risks.

Speed matters less than consistency. Manufacturing, compliance, and safety protocols often benefit from hierarchy because it enforces standardization. When doing things the same way every time is more important than doing them fast, hierarchical control adds value.

You're scaling rapidly and need structure to onboard newcomers. Clear reporting lines and defined roles help new employees understand where they fit. Too much ambiguity creates anxiety and slow integration.

Crisis requires centralized decision-making. When you need to move fast under extreme pressure with imperfect information, distributed consensus doesn't work. Someone needs authority to make the call and commit resources immediately.

Hierarchy fails when:

Innovation requires speed and experimentation. Rigid structures slow adaptation. Markets change faster than approval chains move.

Context matters more than consistency. When every situation requires judgment, not just protocol, frontline expertise beats hierarchical control.

Trust is high and competence is distributed. If you have capable people who trust each other, hierarchy adds friction without adding value.

The work is knowledge-intensive. Creative and analytical work suffers under micro-management. People need autonomy to think, and hierarchy often constrains that autonomy.

The key is matching structure to need, not defaulting to hierarchy because it feels safe or familiar.

Chapter 4
Hierarchy Doesn't Guarantee Results

The Leader I Became

Looking back over two decades, the evolution in my thinking about hierarchy mirrors my evolution as a leader.

Early in my career, I chased titles because I thought they'd give me authority. They did, but only the shallow kind, where people comply because they have to, not because they want to.

Mid-career, I learned that authority unearned by capability is authority resented. I worked to build credibility so the title matched the respect.

Later, I discovered that the highest form of leadership isn't about concentrating authority in yourself, it's about distributing it to others. Not because you're abdicating responsibility, but because you're multiplying impact.

The CFO who told me on my first day that I'd be "responsible for things you never imagined" wasn't warning me about scope creep. He was inviting me to understand that real leadership happens in the gaps between the boxes on the org chart, in the spaces where formal authority ends and personal initiative begins.

The question nobody asked in Jersey City—the one I nervously raised about role clarity, wasn't important because I was brave. It was important because someone needed to speak up, and my lack of hierarchical position freed me to do it.

These lessons don't mean hierarchy is always wrong. They mean hierarchy is a tool, not a philosophy. Use it when it serves the work. Abandon it when it doesn't.

The organizations that thrive understand this. They create structures that provide clarity without creating rigidity. They grant authority based on context and competence, not just seniority. They celebrate people who step up, not just those who wait to be told.

And most importantly, they measure leaders not by how much authority they accumulate, but by how much capability they build in others.

Actions for Readers: Leading Beyond Your Title

Hierarchy is seductive because it's simple, clear lines, defined roles, explicit authority. But simplicity isn't the same as effectiveness. Here's how to build influence that transcends your position:

The Influence Test

Run the empty chair experiment. Skip your next team meeting if your presence isn't essential. Does the team move forward confidently, or stall? The answer reveals whether you've built capability or dependency.

Three Moves This Week:

Ask instead of tell. Before giving your opinion this week, ask three people for theirs. Listen genuinely, not just to be polite. Then incorporate what you hear into your decision. You'll be surprised how often their answer is better than yours.

Give away one decision. Identify one decision you'd normally make yourself. Give it to someone else completely. Don't just delegate the work; give them the actual decision authority. Tell them your decision criteria and boundaries, then step back.

Walk the floor. Spend 30 minutes this week in informal conversations with people you don't normally interact with. Don't ask for status updates. Ask: "What's broken that I don't know about?" and "What would you change if you had authority to do it?" Then help them get that authority.

Chapter 4
Hierarchy Doesn't Guarantee Results

Building Distributed Authority (Choose One This Month):

Create decision rights clarity. For your team's top five recurring decisions, map out explicitly: Who provides input? Who has veto rights? Who ultimately decides? Post this publicly. You'll eliminate hours of "checking with leadership" because people will know they already have authority.

Celebrate upward delegation. When someone solves a problem without escalating it to you, recognize it publicly.

Eliminate one approval layer. Find a category of decisions that currently requires your sign-off. Define clear criteria, then push authority down. Example: "Any expense under $X with clear business justification can be approved by team leads. I trust your judgment."

The Long Game (This Quarter):

Design one area where you're currently the bottleneck to work completely without you. Define the outcome criteria, clarify boundaries, train judgment, document decision frameworks, then step back completely for 30 days. Measure: Did it work? What improved? What broke? What did you learn about where your presence adds value vs. where it creates dependency?

A Closing Reflection

Ten years after that Finance Executive Committee meeting in Jersey City, I ran into the regional CFO who'd thanked me for asking the question nobody else asked.

"Do you remember what you told me that day?" I asked him.

He laughed. "That I should have asked the question myself?"

"You said I had the freedom to ask because I had no title to protect," I said. "At the time, I thought that was a liability. Now I realize it was a gift."

He nodded slowly. "I've thought about that moment a lot. I had the authority but not the courage. You had the courage but not the authority. In that room, you had more influence than any of us."

That's the paradox of hierarchy: often, the people with the most formal authority are the most constrained by it.

They have something to lose, so they play it safe. They have a position to protect, so they don't speak uncomfortable truths. They have a title that grants them permission to lead, but that same title constrains how boldly they can lead.

The real power in organizations doesn't flow from the org chart. It flows from people willing to take responsibility beyond their role, to speak truth without permission, to build capability in others instead of hoarding authority for themselves.

Hierarchy gives you a platform. The real choice lies in how you use the platform. It can consolidate control, or it can distribute capability. That choice defines whether you manage a structure or lead people.

The choice is yours. But remember: people don't follow positions for long. They follow people who help them succeed, who trust them to lead, and who build organizations where influence matters more than hierarchy.

That's leadership that lasts.

Part 2
Building What Lasts : Systems that work without you

Chapter 5
Listening Is A Leadership Superpower

"They say he's an extraordinary listener."

The Conversation I Thought I Understood

Forty-five minutes into a meeting with an insurance company CEO, I realized I'd completely misread the room.

We were there to discuss transforming their finance function—a significant multi-year opportunity. I'd prepared extensively: researched their business, analyzed competitors, developed a compelling modernization vision.

The CEO was polite, attentive, asking clarifying questions. My team nodded along, pleased with our progress. By conventional measures, the meeting was going well.

But something felt off.

His questions weren't challenging, they were careful. His tone wasn't engaged, it was patient. And as I paused to take a breath, I caught something in his expression: resignation, not excitement.

I stopped mid-sentence.

"I'm not sure I'm answering the question you actually have," I said. "What are you really concerned about?"

The room went quiet. My team looked uncomfortable—we were supposed to be in presentation mode, not therapy session mode.

The CEO leaned back and was silent for what felt like an eternity but was probably ten seconds. Then he said: "You've shown me a sophisticated vision for transformation. It's impressive. But what I actually need to know is whether you understand the political minefield I'm navigating internally. I have three business unit heads who don't trust finance, a board that's risk-averse, and a recent failed technology implementation that's made everyone skeptical of change."

Everything shifted in that moment.

For forty-five minutes, I'd been answering the question I wanted him to ask, the one about our technical capabilities and strategic vision. He'd been waiting patiently for me to address the question he actually had: Can you help me navigate the human and political challenges that will make or break this transformation?

I closed my laptop.

"Tell me more about the failed technology implementation," I said.

For the next hour, we barely touched my prepared presentation. Instead, I asked questions. I listened and learned about the relationships, politics, and fears that would ultimately determine whether a well-designed transformation could succeed.

By the end of the meeting, we had a very different proposal than the one I'd walked in with. Less about technical modernization, more about change management and trust-building. Less about what we'd do, more about how we'd do it with the organization's unique dynamics in mind.

We won the engagement. More importantly, I learned something that would transform how I thought about leadership: I wasn't listening, I was waiting to talk.

The Difference Between Hearing and Understanding

That insurance company meeting exposed a pattern I'd been blind to for years: I'd confused hearing with listening.

Hearing is passive. Sound waves hit your ears, your brain processes language, and you register words.

Listening is active, you're trying to understand not just the words, but the meaning beneath them, the concerns driving them, the context shaping them.

I'd been hearing people my entire career. But I'd been listening far less than I thought.

The evidence was everywhere once I started paying attention. In meetings, I'd form my response while others were still talking. I'd interrupt with "solutions" before fully understanding problems. I'd ask questions that were really statements in disguise: "Have you considered...?" (meaning: here's what you should do).

One of my direct reports finally called me out on it.

We were in a one-on-one discussing a client issue. She was explaining the complexity of the situation when I jumped in with a suggestion. She stopped mid-sentence, looked at me directly, and said: "You're not listening. You're solving. And you don't understand the problem yet."

I felt defensive. Of course I was listening. I'd just offered her a solution, hadn't I?

But she was right. I'd heard the surface issue and jumped to fix it without understanding the deeper dynamics. My "solution" would have made things worse because it didn't account for context I hadn't bothered to grasp.

"What am I missing?" I asked, forcing myself to actually listen to the answer instead of preparing my next response.

What she told me over the next twenty minutes completely reframed my understanding of the situation. The "client issue" wasn't actually about the client, it was about internal misalignment on our team. The client was just the symptom. If I'd implemented my quick solution, I would have addressed the symptom while the real problem festered.

That conversation changed something fundamental in how I approached leadership. Problems aren't what people say on the surface—they're what emerges when you genuinely listen beneath the surface.

The Cost of Not Listening

I'll close this chapter with a cautionary story—a time when I failed to listen and paid a significant price.

We were implementing a new performance management system. HR had designed it carefully, consulting best practices, benchmarking against other firms. On paper, it was sound.

But when we rolled it out, resistance was immediate and strong. Managers complained it was too complex. Employees felt it was arbitrary. The process that was supposed to improve performance became a bureaucratic burden everyone resented.

In leadership meetings, I defended the system. "Change is always uncomfortable," I said. "People will adapt. We just need to hold firm."

Six months in, it was clear the system wasn't working. Performance conversations weren't happening, or they were happening purely as compliance exercises. The tool we'd built to improve performance was actually undermining it.

Finally, one of my peers pulled me aside: "You're not listening. People have been telling you this isn't working from day one. But you keep defending it instead of learning why it's broken."

He was right. I'd been so invested in the system—and so convinced that resistance was just typical change aversion—that I'd stopped listening to what people were actually saying.

We eventually scrapped the system and started over, this time beginning with listening: What do managers actually need from a performance tool? What makes performance conversations valuable versus performative? What gets in the way of honest feedback?

The second version was simpler, more flexible, and actually used—because we'd listened before building, not after.

That failure cost us six months and significant organizational goodwill. More importantly, it taught me that when smart people are telling you something isn't working, the problem is usually not their resistance—it's your listening.

When I Finally Stopped Talking First

The hardest part about learning to listen wasn't developing new techniques. It was overcoming a lifetime of training that had taught me the opposite.

From school through my entire career, I'd been rewarded for having answers, not asking questions. For speaking confidently, not listening carefully. For demonstrating expertise, not acknowledging uncertainty.

The people who got promoted were the ones who could walk into a room and command it with their ideas. The ones who could present with authority. The ones who could "take charge" of conversations.

Listening felt passive by comparison. Weak, even. Like I wasn't adding value if I wasn't talking.

But I started experimenting with a different approach.

In a team meeting where we were wrestling with a strategic direction, I held back from offering my view. Instead, I asked questions. I invited perspectives. I sat with the discomfort of not being the one with the answer.

Chapter 5
Listening Is A Leadership Superpower

The first fifteen minutes were awkward. People kept looking to me to break the impasse. I could feel their expectation: "You're the leader. Tell us what to do."

I stayed quiet.

Eventually, someone tentatively offered a perspective. Then someone else built on it. What followed was a genuine, substantive debate—not a performative one—where ideas got tested. Assumptions got challenged. The conversation went places I couldn't have directed it.

By the end of the meeting, the team had developed a strategic approach I wouldn't have thought of, and because they'd developed it together, their commitment to executing it was far stronger than if I'd just told them what to do.

Afterward, one team member pulled me aside: "That was the first time I felt like my opinion actually mattered in a strategy conversation. Usually you come in with the answer already formed, and we're just validating it."

The feedback landed hard. But it was true.

I'd been using meetings to get buy-in for my ideas, not to generate better ideas through collective thinking. I'd been hearing objections as obstacles to overcome, not as information to integrate.

But not talking wasn't enough. I had to learn when to stay silent—even when silence felt uncomfortable.

The Power of Uncomfortable Silence

Six months after I started practicing active listening, I faced a test that revealed how far I'd come, and how much further I had to go.

We were debating whether to acquire a smaller competitor. The financial case was marginal. The strategic logic was sound but not overwhelming. The team was split.

In the meeting, people made their cases. Some advocated for the acquisition, citing market share gains and talent acquisition. Others argued against it, pointing to integration risks and cultural misalignment.

I had a strong opinion. The acquisition felt like a distraction, expensive, risky, and not clearly aligned with our core strategy. I wanted to say no.

But I'd learned that my strong opinions often shut down conversation too quickly. So I decided to try something different: I stayed completely silent.

Not just quiet, deliberately, visibly silent. People made their arguments. Debated each other. Looked to me for a signal. I gave none.

The silence became uncomfortable. People started shifting in their seats. Someone asked directly: "What do you think we should do?"

I said: "I'm not sure yet. Keep going."

Something interesting happened in that discomfort. The conversation got more honest.

One person who'd been advocating for the acquisition suddenly said: "Look, if I'm being completely honest, I'm not sure this is the right move. I've been arguing for it because I worked on the business case, but the more I hear the concerns, the more I wonder if we're rationalizing a decision we want to make rather than a decision we should make."

That admission opened the floodgates. Others started voicing doubts they'd been holding back. The conversation shifted from advocacy to genuine inquiry. By staying silent, I'd created space for people to think out loud, to change their minds, to voice uncertainty without it feeling like weakness.

After ninety minutes, we reached a decision, not to pursue the acquisition. But more importantly, everyone owned that decision because they'd genuinely wrestled with it, not because I'd told them what to do.

I practiced this technique deliberately. In management meetings, instead of immediately responding to proposals, I'd count to ten before speaking. In performance reviews, after delivering feedback, I'd simply wait, letting the other person process before rushing to fill the space.

The discomfort was mine to manage, not theirs. And what emerged in that space was often more valuable than anything I could have said.

The most powerful listening tool I discovered was the question that opens up thinking rather than shuts it down.

The Art of the Question

For most of my career, I thought I was good at asking questions. I wasn't. I was good at disguising advice as questions.

"Have you considered trying X?" (Translation: You should try X.)

"Don't you think it would be better to Y?" (Translation: Do Y.)

"What if we approached it this way?" (Translation: Here's the approach I want.)

These aren't questions, they're suggestions wearing a question mark as camouflage. And people see right through them.

Lead Less, Build More

Real questions open up thinking rather than channeling it toward your preferred answer. They create space for discovery rather than merely confirming what you already believe.

I learned the difference between advocacy and inquiry the hard way.

In most meetings, I'd been trained to advocate, state my view, make my case, defend my position. I'd been rewarded my whole career for having answers, for knowing the right direction. Inquiry felt like weakness, like I didn't have conviction.

Then I read Chris Argyris and Donald Schön's work on organizational learning, and something clicked: advocacy without inquiry creates echo chambers. People nod along not because they agree, but because challenging you feels unsafe.

But genuine inquiry, asking questions that explore how others think, opens up possibilities you'd never see through advocacy alone.

I started paying attention to the questions I asked and realized most of them were closed, leading, or thinly disguised solutions:

"Why didn't you...?" (implies they should have) "Don't you think...?" (disguised advocacy) "Have you considered...?" (advice masked as question) "What were you thinking?" (rarely asked genuinely) "Wouldn't it be better to...?" (judgment disguised as curiosity)

These questions don't invite thinking, they invite defensiveness.

I started experimenting with genuinely open questions:

"What's most important to you about this?" "What would success look like?" "What concerns you most?" "What am I missing?" "What else should I be asking?"

The difference was immediate. People's body language changed. Instead of bracing for judgment, they leaned in. Instead of defending decisions, they explored complexity. Instead of giving me the answer they thought I wanted, they shared what they actually thought.

Why Listening Doesn't Stop at the First "Why"

Most leaders think listening ends when someone answers the question. It doesn't. The first answer is rarely the real one. It's the most defensible one.

Real listening means staying curious long enough for people to move past explanations that protect them—and toward truths that can actually change something.

That's where the Five Whys comes in. This technique transformed how I approached problem-solving: Toyota's Five Whys.

The concept is simple: when you encounter a problem, ask "why?" five times to get past symptoms to root causes.

Problem: We missed the delivery deadline. Why? The testing phase took longer than expected. Why? We found critical bugs late in the process. Why? Testing didn't start until development was complete. Why? Testers weren't involved in the design phase. Why? We don't have a process for early tester engagement.

Root cause: Process design, not execution failure.

The brilliance of Five Whys isn't the number five—it's the discipline of not stopping at the first, most obvious answer.

I used this technique in a situation that was generating significant client frustration. We kept missing deliverables for a major engagement. The project manager blamed resource constraints. Fair enough—we were stretched thin. I could have just assigned more people.

But instead, I asked why.

Why are we missing deliverables? "We don't have enough people on this project."

Why don't we have enough people? "Because several team members were pulled to other urgent projects."

Why were they pulled? "Because those projects were in crisis mode."

Why were multiple projects in crisis mode simultaneously? "Because we're saying yes to aggressive timelines we can't realistically meet."

Why are we saying yes to unrealistic timelines? "Because we're afraid of losing deals if we push back on client expectations."

Now we were getting somewhere. The problem wasn't resource constraints, it was our sales process setting unrealistic expectations, which created downstream crises, which forced resource reallocation, which undermined delivery on other projects.

Throwing more people at the original project wouldn't have solved anything. It would have depleted resources from yet another project, creating a new crisis.

The Five Whys revealed that we needed to fix our sales-to-delivery handoff, not our staffing levels.

That one conversation, driven by systematic questioning, saved us from making an expensive mistake and pointed us toward the real solution.

Chapter 5
Listening Is A Leadership Superpower

The Five Whys didn't give us better answers. It permitted us to listen longer, without defending, fixing, or deflecting. And that changed everything.

When Listening Reveals What Data Hides

The most profound lessons about listening came from situations where the data said one thing but listening revealed something completely different.

A colleague once shared an experience from a hospital consulting engagement. Surgical error rates remained high despite excellent surgeons and modern facilities, and the Chief Medical Officer initially assumed the problem was technical.

But observing actual surgeries revealed something else. Technical execution was sound. Communication was broken.

In one case, a nurse noticed a potential medication interaction but hesitated to speak up. The surgeon had a reputation for dismissing concerns. By the time she finally raised the issue, they were mid-procedure. The delay created risk that shouldn't have existed.

This pattern repeated across multiple teams. Edmondson's psychological safety research found that teams reporting the most errors weren't making more mistakes—they were being more honest. Low-safety teams hid problems until they became crises.

The hospital's high error rates weren't actually a problem, they were a symptom. The real problem was that people didn't feel safe speaking up early, so small concerns escalated into major events.

No amount of additional training or technology would have fixed that. What they needed was cultural change that made it safe to raise concerns, the kind of change that only happens when leaders listen to what people are reluctant to say.

Two years into my listening experiments, I faced perhaps my biggest test.

We were holding a strategy session with senior leadership to set priorities for the next fiscal year. As the most senior operational leader, everyone expected me to drive the conversation.

I decided not to.

I opened the meeting with three questions:

1. What's working that we should do more of?
2. What's not working that we should stop?
3. What are we not doing that we should start?

Then I sat back and facilitated, but I didn't advocate. For three hours, I asked questions, invited quieter voices, paraphrased to ensure understanding, but never stated my own view.

It was excruciating. Multiple times, I wanted to jump in with my perspective. I had opinions. I had ideas. But I held back.

By the end of the session, the team had developed a strategic framework I hadn't anticipated, and it was better than what I would have proposed. More importantly, the buy-in was complete because everyone had contributed to shaping it.

Afterward, one of my peers said: "I've never seen you lead like that before. It felt like you weren't leading at all."

"Exactly," I said. "That was the point."

The Listening Toolkit

Beyond the silence and inquiry techniques I've described, here are three additional practices that transformed my listening:

The Repeat-Back: Before responding to any proposal or concern, restate what you heard in your own words: "Let me make sure I understand—you're saying..." This forces you to process before reacting and shows the other person you're genuinely trying to understand.

The Summarize-and-Check: In longer conversations, pause periodically to summarize: "So far I'm hearing three main concerns..." Then ask: "What am I missing?" This catches misunderstandings early and often surfaces what people were holding back.

The Directional Question: The better question isn't 'What should we do?', but 'What matters most here?' This surfaces values and priorities that inform better solutions later.

The Listening Ladder

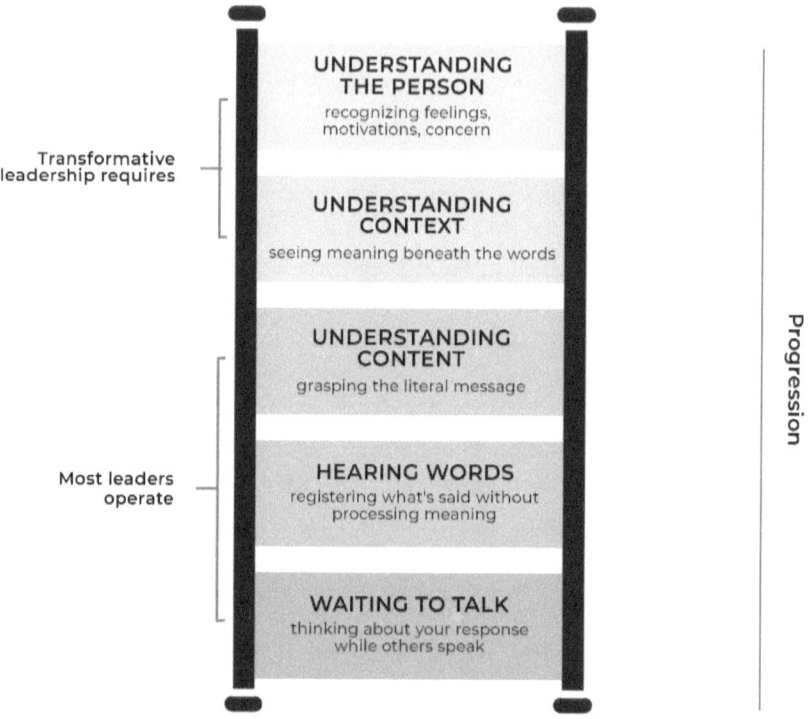

Listening isn't a binary skill-it's a spectrum. Moving up the ladder requires deliberate practice and discomfort

Listening isn't a binary skill—it's a spectrum. Moving up the ladder requires deliberate practice and discomfort.

The Practice of Speaking Last

One technique became my most powerful listening tool: deliberately speaking last in meetings.

Chapter 5
Listening Is A Leadership Superpower

Not just holding back my opinion, structurally putting myself at the end of the conversation.

I started doing this in our weekly leadership team meetings. Instead of opening with the agenda and my framing, I'd ask someone else to frame the issue. Then I'd facilitate discussion, asking questions, drawing out perspectives, but not offering my own view until everyone else had spoken.

The first few times, it was awkward. People kept looking to me for signals. "What do you think?" they'd ask midway through.

"I'm not sure yet," I'd say. "I want to hear everyone's thinking first."

Eventually, they stopped looking to me for validation mid-conversation. They started debating each other, testing ideas, building on each other's thoughts. The quality of discussion improved because people weren't calibrating their responses to match what they thought I wanted to hear.

And when I finally did speak at the end, my perspective was better informed. I'd heard angles I wouldn't have considered. I'd learned about concerns I didn't know existed. My final synthesis was stronger because it integrated everyone's thinking rather than simply imposing mine.

One caution: speaking last only works if you genuinely listen. If people sense you're humoring them before announcing your pre-formed decision, the technique backfires. They'll stop contributing because they know their input doesn't matter.

The commitment has to be real: I will let this conversation shape my thinking, even if it means changing my mind.

When Listening Saved a Relationship

I learned this most painfully in my own team. In an earlier chapter, I described how a senior project manager I trusted nearly disengaged—not because of her performance, but because she felt unheard and mistrusted. What changed that situation wasn't a new system or role clarity. It was listening without diagnosis, without defense, and without agenda.

The Questions That Open Up Thinking

The difference between good and great questions became clearer the more I practiced.

Closed questions shut down thinking:

- "Did you consider option A?" (yes/no answer)
- "Is the project on track?" (invites performance theater)
- "Do you agree with this approach?" (forces binary choice)

Open questions expand thinking:

- "What options are you weighing?" (reveals their thought process)
- "What's your biggest concern about the timeline?" (surfaces real issues)
- "What would change your mind about this approach?" (tests conviction)

But the most powerful questions do something more: they help people think better, not just share what they've already thought.

Questions that expand perspective:

- "If you were in their position, how would you see this?"
- "What would need to be true for this to work?"
- "What are we not seeing because we're too close to it?"

Questions that test assumptions:

- "What are we assuming that might not be true?"

- "What would happen if we did the opposite?"
- "What would someone from outside this industry ask?"

Questions that surface values:

- "What matters most to you about this decision?"
- "What would we regret not doing?"
- "Ten years from now, what will we wish we had known?"

I started keeping a list of powerful questions and deliberately using them in high-stakes conversations. The impact was remarkable, not because the questions were clever, but because they genuinely helped people think more clearly.

The Listening Culture I Tried to Build

Individual listening practices matter. But if you're in a leadership position, your real opportunity is building a culture where listening becomes the norm, not the exception.

Here's what that looked like in practice:

We changed how meetings started. Instead of diving into agendas, we began with: "What questions do we need to answer in this meeting?" This shifted focus from information-sharing to genuine problem-solving.

We changed how meetings ended. Instead of assuming alignment, we closed with: "What didn't get said that should have been said?" This created space for people to voice concerns they'd been holding back.

We celebrated great questions. When someone asked a question that reframed the conversation, I highlighted it: "That question just changed how I'm thinking about this. Thank you." Over time, people learned that asking penetrating questions was as valued as having smart answers.

We practiced the repeat-back. Before any major decision, we required two people—not the decision owner—to restate the decision in their own words. If they couldn't, or if their versions differed, we didn't have clarity yet.

We made silence okay. I modeled being comfortable with pauses in conversation. When someone needed time to think, we waited. When a question hung in the air unanswered, we let it hang rather than rushing to fill the space.

The cultural shift was gradual but measurable. In employee surveys, scores for "I feel heard by leadership" rose from 62% to 89% over three years. More importantly, the quality of execution improved because problems surfaced early when they were still manageable.

Actions for Readers: Becoming a Listening Leader

Listening isn't a technique you learn once, it's a practice you refine constantly. Here's how to start:

The 7-Day Listening Challenge:

Day 1: Count your questions. Track how many questions you ask vs. statements you make in meetings. Target: 2:1 ratio.

Day 2: Practice the 10-second pause. Before responding to anything, count to 10. Notice what changes.

Day 3: The repeat-back practice. In every conversation, restate what you heard before giving your view.

Day 4: Ask "What else?" three times. When someone answers your question, don't move on—ask "What else?" Three times. See what emerges.

Day 5: Silent meetings. Run one meeting where you speak last—or not at all. Let others lead.

Day 6: The listening audit. Ask three people: "On a scale of 1-10, how well do I listen? What would make it a 10?" Don't defend—just thank them.

Day 7: Review and commit. What did you learn? What will you keep doing?

This Month:

Implement one structural change that forces better listening:

- Start meetings with "What questions do we need to answer?" not "Here's what we're doing"
- End meetings with "What didn't get said that should have been said?"
- Replace one weekly status meeting with 1-on-1 listening sessions

This Quarter:

Build a listening culture:

- Train your team on inquiry vs. advocacy
- Create psychological safety metrics: track how often people voice concerns early
- Celebrate great questions as loudly as you celebrate great answers
- Run the Five Whys exercise on your biggest recurring problem
- Practice speaking last in all strategy discussions for one month

A Closing Reflection

That insurance company CEO meeting from the opening of this chapter changed my career trajectory, not because I made a brilliant presentation, but because I finally stopped presenting long enough to listen.

The transformation we eventually designed for his finance organization succeeded not because of our technical expertise, but because we understood the political and human dynamics that would determine whether change stuck.

I learned that day that leadership isn't about having the best answers, it's about asking the best questions and genuinely listening to the answers.

Ten years later, I still think about that moment when I closed my laptop and said, "Tell me more about the failed technology implementation."

That's the moment leadership actually began, not when I started talking, but when I finally stopped.

The irony of writing about listening is that you're reading my words rather than me listening to yours. But if you take only one thing from this chapter, let it be this:

> *The people you lead know more about what's really happening than you do. Your job isn't to have all the answers. Your job is to create the conditions where truth can be spoken and heard.*

Listening doesn't mean your mind won't wander. It means you notice when it does and choose to return.

Listening doesn't require you to suspend thinking or agreement. It requires you to suspend certainty long enough to understand.

That work begins with genuine, patient listening, particularly when what you hear is uncomfortable.

Chapter 6
Clarity over Consensus

The Meeting That Looked Perfect

The quarterly quality review looked like every other executive meeting I'd attended that year. Polished slides. Confident presenters. A dashboard full of green indicators showing everything was "on track."

I was sitting in as an observer, invited by the COO who wanted an outside perspective on their quality management process. Around the table sat functional heads from engineering, operations, client services, and product—all nodding along as the quality director walked through the metrics.

"Client satisfaction: 87%, up 3 points from last quarter. Green."
"Defect rates: within acceptable thresholds. Green."
"Process compliance: 94%. Green."
"Delivery timelines: 89% on schedule. Green."

Green. Green. Green. Everything was fine. Everyone seemed satisfied.

But something felt off. I'd been consulting long enough to recognize the signs of a well-rehearsed performance. The metrics were suspiciously tidy. The trends were conveniently positive. And most tellingly, nobody was asking hard questions.

Halfway through the presentation, I raised my hand.

"Can you help me understand what's behind the client satisfaction number? You said 87%—what does that actually mean? How many clients? What were they asked? What did the other 13% say?"

The quality director paused. "We survey clients quarterly using our standard satisfaction parameters."

"Right, but what does 87% satisfied mean? Are they thrilled or just not unhappy? What feedback are we getting that doesn't show up in that number?"

Another pause. "The survey asks them to rate us on a five-point scale. 87% gave us a 4 or 5."

"So 13% gave you 3 or below. What did they say when you followed up with them?"

Chapter 6
Clarity over Consensus

Silence.

"We don't typically follow up on individual responses. The aggregate data is what we track."

I pressed further. "And the defect rates, you said within acceptable thresholds. What's the threshold? Who set it? What's the trend over the past four quarters, not just this one?"

The room temperature dropped noticeably. The quality director was now visibly uncomfortable. Other executives were shifting in their seats.

What emerged over the next thirty minutes was a complete disconnect between the dashboard and reality. The "acceptable threshold" for defects had been set years ago and never revisited. Client satisfaction had been trending down for six quarters but still looked "green" because the threshold was low. Several major client escalations from the past month weren't reflected in any of the metrics because they were categorized as "one-time issues."

The dashboard was green. The reality was concerning. And everyone in that room had been nodding along because consensus, everyone agreeing that things looked fine, felt safer than clarity about what was actually happening.

Earlier, I described how my addiction to consensus created fragmentation in execution. This chapter is about what I learned to do instead: prioritize clarity over comfort, and speed over unanimous agreement.

Why Consensus Fails

For most of my career, I'd been taught that consensus was the hallmark of good leadership. Get everyone in the room. Hear all perspectives. Build agreement. Don't move forward until everyone is on board.

It sounds collaborative. It feels inclusive. And it's often a recipe for mediocrity and delay.

The problem with consensus isn't that input is bad. Input is essential. The problem is that consensus optimizes for agreement rather than for truth, and for comfort rather than for action.

When consensus becomes the goal, several dysfunctions emerge:

The loudest voices dominate. Not the smartest or most informed—the most persistent. People who care about being right more than being effective shape the outcome because they'll outlast everyone else

Truth gets softened. To achieve consensus, you round off the sharp edges of reality. "This is concerning" becomes "This is something to monitor." "We're failing" becomes "We're facing challenges." Language gets polished until everyone can agree, which often means it no longer reflects reality.

Decisions get delayed. When you need everyone on board, the timeline extends to accommodate the slowest person to align. "Let me think about it" becomes a veto, even if the person saying it has the least context.

Accountability diffuses. When everyone agrees, everyone is responsible, which means no one is. If something fails, people point to the group consensus: "We all decided this together." Individual ownership disappears.

Speed dies. Consensus is inherently slow. Every perspective must be heard. Every concern must be addressed. Every objection must be resolved. In fast-moving environments, the time spent building consensus becomes a competitive disadvantage.

I watched this play out painfully during a product development cycle. We spent six weeks building consensus on feature prioritization. Every team had input. Every concern was addressed. Everyone finally agreed.

By the time we launched, a competitor had already released a similar product. Our window had closed. The product failed not because our features were wrong, it failed because while we were perfecting consensus, the market moved on.

The hard truth I had to learn: clarity beats consensus. Speed beats unanimity. Decisive action with 70% agreement outperforms perfect alignment that comes too late.

The Directly Responsible Individual (DRI)

The concept of the Directly Responsible Individual, or DRI, originated at Apple. In meetings, Steve Jobs would simply ask, 'Who's the DRI?' If no one could answer immediately, the meeting ended.

The logic: committees diffuse responsibility. When everyone is responsible, no one is. A DRI changes this. One person owns the outcome, gathers input, decides, delivers. If it fails, there's no ambiguity about who answers for it.

I started implementing DRIs systematically, and the organizational impact was immediate.

For product launches, instead of a "launch committee," we had a launch DRI. They owned the timeline, coordinated cross-functional work, and made final calls on readiness.

For client escalations, instead of "joint accountability," we named an escalation DRI who owned the resolution path and kept all stakeholders informed.

For strategic initiatives, instead of steering committees that "oversaw" progress, we had initiative DRIs who drove outcomes and reported on them.

The shift was subtle but profound. People stopped waiting for group agreement and started driving toward outcomes. Meetings became shorter because we weren't building consensus, we were informing a DRI who'd make the call.

The clearest example came during a major systems migration. We'd been "planning" for months with a cross-functional team. Lots of meetings, lots of input, no real progress.

I named a senior engineer as the single DRI for the entire migration. Not the team or the steering committee. One person.

Within two weeks, decisions that had been stalled for months were made. He consulted broadly, but he decided quickly. When conflicts arose, he resolved them instead of scheduling another meeting to discuss them.

The migration completed six weeks ahead of the original timeline. When I asked him what changed, he said: "Before, I thought my job was to facilitate agreement. Once I knew I was accountable for the outcome, I stopped optimizing for consensus and started optimizing for success."

That's the power of the DRI: it converts collaborative paralysis into decisive action.

The Repeat-Back Test

Naming a DRI creates accountability. But accountability without clarity is just blame waiting to happen. The second tool I learned was deceptively simple: before any meeting ends, have two people restate the decision in their own words.

In a marketing strategy meeting, after ninety minutes of debate, everyone seemed aligned. Before adjourning, I asked two people to restate our positioning decision.

Chapter 6
Clarity over Consensus

The first person: "We're emphasizing speed and efficiency."

The second person: "We're emphasizing quality and expertise."

Same meeting. Opposite conclusions. We didn't have a decision, we had an illusion of agreement.

This happened more often than I wanted to admit. We'd have intense discussions, people would nod along, and we'd leave thinking we were aligned. Days or weeks later, we'd discover teams were executing completely different interpretations of the "decision."

The repeat-back test solves this. It's uncomfortable because it exposes when consensus was performance rather than genuine understanding. But that discomfort is far cheaper than the cost of discovering misalignment weeks into execution.

I made it standard practice: every decision-making meeting ends with the five-point close-out:

1. **Summarize the decision in one sentence.** If you can't, you don't have a decision yet.
2. **Name the DRI and first milestone.** Who owns it? What's the first deliverable?
3. **Define what "done" means.** Not "make progress"—what does complete look like?
4. **State what we're NOT doing.** Boundaries matter as much as direction.
5. **Repeat-back test with two people.** Can they restate it identically?

If the repeat-back fails, if people give different answers, the meeting isn't over. We keep talking until we have genuine clarity.

Lead Less, Build More

Disagree and Commit

Clarity doesn't require agreement. This was perhaps the hardest lesson to internalize.

For years, I'd thought my job as a leader was to build consensus before moving forward. If people disagreed, I needed to keep working until everyone got on board. Disagreement felt like failure.

But Amazon's "disagree and commit" principle reframed my thinking entirely. You can disagree with a decision and still commit fully to executing it. In fact, that's often the sign of organizational maturity.

Jeff Bezos articulated it clearly: "Have backbone; disagree and commit. Leaders are obligated to respectfully challenge decisions when they disagree, even when doing so is uncomfortable or exhausting. Leaders have conviction and are tenacious. They do not compromise for the sake of social cohesion. Once a decision is determined, they commit wholly."

I saw this principle transform our executive team dynamics.

We were debating a significant investment in a new service line. I was skeptical—the business case felt thin, the market timing uncertain. I made my concerns clear in the debate.

But after thorough discussion, the CEO decided to move forward. The moment he made that call, I had a choice: keep lobbying for my position, or disagree and commit.

I chose commit.

In the next leadership meeting, when someone asked about the new service line, I didn't say "Well, I had concerns but we're doing it anyway." I said: "We're moving forward with the investment. Here's why it makes strategic sense, and here's how we're de-risking it."

Chapter 6
Clarity over Consensus

My private disagreement didn't disappear. But my public commitment was complete.

Eighteen months later, the service line became one of our fastest-growing offerings. My initial skepticism had been wrong. But even if I'd been right, committing fully to execution would have given the initiative its best chance to succeed.

Disagree and commit works because it separates decision-making from execution. You can debate fiercely, advocate for your position, and challenge assumptions during the decision phase. But once a decision is made, fragmented execution helps no one.

The cultural shift this created was profound. People stopped viewing disagreement as disloyalty. They voiced concerns more openly because they knew disagreement during debate was valued. But they also stopped sabotaging decisions they disagreed with, because commitment after decisions was expected.

The Pre-Mortem

One tool that dramatically improved our decision quality was the pre-mortem, a technique I learned from psychologist Gary Klein.

Standard practice: make a decision, execute, review what went wrong if it fails.

Pre-mortem: before executing, assume the decision has failed spectacularly. Work backward to identify what went wrong. Then address those risks proactively.

We used this on a major client engagement where we'd proposed an aggressive timeline. Everyone was confident. The plan looked solid.

Before kicking off, I gathered the team: "It's six months from now. The engagement has been a disaster. The client is threatening to terminate the contract. What happened?"

The room shifted from confident to contemplative. People started surfacing concerns they'd been holding back:

"We didn't account for their internal approval cycles being slower than ours." "Our technical assumptions about their systems integration turned out to be wrong." "The client SMEs we're counting on aren't actually available full-time like they promised." "We have three team members who've never worked together—personality conflicts could derail collaboration."

None of these concerns had surfaced in our planning meetings when we were in "make it work" mode. But the pre-mortem created permission to voice doubt.

We addressed every concern before starting. We built buffer into timelines. We validated technical assumptions early. We confirmed SME availability and had backup plans. We facilitated team dynamics conversations upfront.

The engagement didn't fail. In fact, it exceeded expectations. Not because our original plan was perfect, because the pre-mortem helped us see and address weaknesses before they became crises.

The Forcing Function

Speed often requires manufactured urgency. Without deadlines that force decisions, discussions can circle endlessly.

I learned to use forcing functions deliberately, constraints that made clarity unavoidable.

Chapter 6
Clarity over Consensus

The public commitment. Announce the decision date publicly before making the decision. "We'll decide by Friday and communicate to the organization Monday." Now you can't punt.

The reversible pilot. Instead of debating whether something will work, commit to trying it for a defined period: "We'll test this approach for 30 days, measure results, then decide whether to continue." This converts "should we?" debates into "let's learn" experiments.

The decision meeting. Not a discussion meeting, a decision meeting. Agenda is clear: we're deciding X today. Input is welcome. Consensus is not required. Someone will make the call before we leave this room.

I used this on a product launch that had been "nearly ready" for three months. Engineering wanted one more sprint to polish features. Marketing wanted more time to refine positioning. Sales wanted to wait for a major industry conference two months away.

We were "almost there" indefinitely.

I called a decision meeting: We're in this room for two hours. By the end, we will have a launch date. Period. Bring your input, but we're leaving with a decision."

Two hours later: launch date set for six weeks out. Not perfect, but clear. The product launched successfully because everyone had six weeks of focused execution instead of perpetual preparation.

The Six Tools Recap

Here are the decision-making tools that transformed how we operated:

Tool 1: The DRI (Directly Responsible Individual) - One person owns the outcome, not a committee. They gather input but they decide and deliver.

Tool 2: The Repeat-Back Test - Before any meeting ends, two people restate the decision. If they give different answers, you don't have clarity yet.

Tool 3: Disagree and Commit - Voice your concerns during debate. Commit fully to execution once decided. Fragmented commitment helps no one.

Tool 4: The Pre-Mortem - Before executing, assume it failed. Work backward to identify what went wrong. Address those risks now.

Tool 5: The Forcing Function - Create constraints that make decisions unavoidable: public commitments, time-boxed pilots, decision meetings (not discussion meetings).

Tool 6: Demand Artifacts, Not Adjectives - Replace status language with evidence: what shipped (with links), what's next (with dates). This simple shift from "on track" to "here's the link" eliminates most status theater and forces clarity about actual progress.

When Clarity Fails

Clarity isn't always the answer. I learned this when we over-rotated on decisiveness and created new problems.

We launched a new product with crystal-clear positioning, aggressive timelines, and a named DRI. No ambiguity. No committee decisions. Pure clarity and speed.

It failed spectacularly.

Why?

Because we'd optimized for clarity about the wrong things. We were clear about what we wanted to build but hadn't validated whether customers wanted it. We were clear about timelines but hadn't tested whether they were realistic. We'd mistaken confidence for correctness.

The post-mortem was humbling. We'd been so proud of our clarity and speed that we'd skipped fundamental questions about product-market fit. Clarity had become its own goal rather than a means to better outcomes.

I learned that clarity works when:

- **You're executing a validated direction.** Clarity accelerates what you know needs to happen.
- **The situation requires speed over perfection.** Some decisions benefit from moving fast and adjusting.
- **Accountability is clear.** Someone owns the outcome and has authority to act.

Clarity fails when:

- **Direction itself is uncertain.** If you don't know where to go, being clear about how to get there doesn't help.
- **Learning matters more than speed.** Sometimes you need exploration, not execution.
- **Context is rapidly changing.** Rigid clarity becomes a liability when circumstances shift.

The art is knowing when to optimize for clarity and when to optimize for learning. Both matter. The mistake is treating every situation as if it requires the same approach.

From Consensus to Clarity: What Changes

After years of experimenting with these tools, here's what the shift from consensus-driven to clarity-driven decision-making actually looks like:

CONSENSUS-DRIVEN:

- Decision-making by committee; everyone must agree
- Timeline driven by slowest person to align
- Accountability diffused across the group
- Conflict avoided to maintain harmony
- Outcome: Agreement (but often fragmented execution)

CLARITY-DRIVEN:

- Decision-making by DRI; input welcomed, consensus not required
- Timeline driven by market need and forcing functions
- Accountability crystal clear—one name
- Conflict surfaced and resolved explicitly
- Outcome: Action (even with disagreement)

This doesn't mean consensus is always wrong. For decisions that require sustained commitment from multiple parties, major cultural changes, shared governance models, building genuine buy-in matters. The goal isn't to eliminate input or collaboration. It's to stop confusing comfort with effectiveness.

Building a Clarity Culture

Individual decision-making practices matter. But cultural transformation happens when these practices become organizational norms.

Here's what that looked like at scale:

We stopped rewarding consensus. When someone made a timely decision with dissenting views, we celebrated it. When someone kept debating past the decision deadline, we called it out as a cultural miss.

We made DRIs visible. Every strategic initiative had a named owner in our central tracker, visible to everyone. Ambiguity about ownership became culturally unacceptable.

We normalized disagree and commit. Leaders modeled it. In all-hands meetings, executives would say: "I disagreed with this decision in the leadership meeting. Here's why I disagreed. But the decision was made, and I'm fully committed to making it work."

We measured clarity, not just consensus. In post-meeting surveys, we asked: "Was the decision clear?" not "Did you agree?" A score of 9-10 on clarity was success, even if agreement was low.

We created space for dissent during decisions, but not after. Before decisions: challenge everything, voice all concerns, debate vigorously. After decisions: commit fully or escalate explicitly, but don't undermine passively.

The culture shift took eighteen months, but the results were measurable. Decision cycle times dropped by 50%. Employee engagement scores for "I know what's expected of me" rose from 71% to 92%. Execution speed increased because people stopped waiting for perfect alignment before acting.

A Closing Story

Five years after that quality committee meeting where the green dashboard masked reality, I found myself in a similar situation, but with a very different outcome.

We were reviewing quarterly results. One team lead presented metrics that looked concerning. Not green. Not "on track." Just honest data showing we were behind on several commitments.

Before I could ask questions, the COO said: "I appreciate the transparency. What do you need from us to close these gaps?"

The team lead outlined specific requests, resources, decisions, removal of blockers. Within fifteen minutes, we'd assigned DRIs to each issue and set clear follow-up dates.

As the meeting ended, the team lead said: "Thank you for not making me spin this. Last company I worked at, if you showed red on a dashboard, you spent more time explaining and defending than actually fixing the problem."

That's when I knew the culture had shifted. We'd stopped rewarding performance theater and started rewarding clarity, even when clarity revealed problems.

Because here's what I learned through all these years of experimentation: consensus feels comfortable, but clarity drives results. Unanimous agreement feels collaborative, but decisive action creates outcomes. Harmony in meetings is nice, but clarity in execution is essential.

The organizations that win aren't the ones where everyone agrees all the time. They're the ones where decisions are clear, ownership is unambiguous, and execution happens fast—even when people disagree.

That's the shift from consensus to clarity. It's uncomfortable. It requires new muscles. It feels less collaborative at first.

But it builds organizations that move fast, execute effectively, and deliver results, which, in the end, is what leadership is actually about.

Chapter 6
Clarity over Consensus

Actions for Readers: From Consensus to Clarity

Examine your last three major decisions. For each, ask:

- Was there a named DRI? (If not, you had a committee, not a decision)
- Could two people restate the decision identically? (If not, you had consensus, not clarity)
- Did you define what you're NOT doing? (If not, you had direction without boundaries)

Score: 3/3 on all three decisions = you're already operating with clarity. Less than that = read on.

This Week - Install Clarity Infrastructure:

In your next meeting where a decision gets made, try the 5-point close-out:

1. One-sentence decision summary
2. Named DRI + first milestone
3. Definition of "done"
4. What we're NOT doing
5. Two-person repeat-back test

Practice "disagree and commit"—voice your disagreement clearly, then commit fully to the decision once it's made.

This Month - Embed Clarity Tools:

Replace one recurring status meeting with an artifacts review:

- No "we're on track" language allowed
- Only "here's what shipped" (with links) and "here's what's next" (with dates)

Run one pre-mortem on your highest-risk initiative:

- Assume it failed spectacularly
- Work backward to identify what went wrong
- Address those risks now

Create decision rights for your top three recurring decision types:

- Who provides input?
- Who has veto power?
- Who decides?

This Quarter - Build Clarity Culture:

Train your team on the six tools from this chapter. Start with DRIs and repeat-back tests.

Measure clarity:

- Track: What % of decisions have named DRIs?
- Track: How often do post-meeting surveys show alignment on what was decided?
- Track: Decision cycle time for standard decisions

Celebrate clarity over consensus:

- When someone makes a clear decision with a dissenting view, recognize it
- When someone says "I disagree but commit," highlight it publicly
- When a meeting ends with perfect clarity, acknowledge that's what good looks like

A Final Reflection

That quality committee meeting taught me something fundamental: consensus is seductive because it feels collaborative, but clarity is essential because it drives action.

Ten years later, I still use every tool in this chapter. The DRI. The repeat-back test. Disagree and commit. The pre-mortem. The forcing function.

Not because they make decisions easier—they often make them harder in the moment. But because they make execution faster, accountability clearer, and outcomes better.

The next time you're in a meeting where everyone is nodding but nothing is clear, remember: agreement isn't the goal. Action is.

And action requires clarity, not consensus.

Chapter 7
Conflict as a Competitive Advantage

"What do you mean you're uncomfortable with conflict?"

The Conversation Nobody Would Have

The steering committee meeting looked productive, polite questions, thoughtful nods, careful phrasing.

We were reviewing a struggling strategic initiative. Timelines had slipped twice. Budget overruns were mounting. The executive sponsor's updates were vague: "encountering challenges," "working through complexity."

Everyone knew it was in trouble. Nobody wanted to say it directly.

Around the table sat senior leaders with decades of experience. People who'd successfully managed complex programs, navigated difficult client relationships, made tough calls under pressure. But in this room, facing this situation, everyone defaulted to diplomatic language that avoided the core issue.

Finally, someone ventured a careful question: "Do we have confidence in the revised timeline?"

The executive sponsor responded with a ten-minute explanation of mitigation strategies, contingency plans, and risk management approaches. It was impressively articulate. It was also a non-answer.

Nobody pushed back.

The meeting ended with polite agreement to "continue monitoring closely" and "revisit in the next review cycle."

Three weeks later, the initiative collapsed entirely. The client terminated the engagement. We wrote off millions in sunk costs. The executive sponsor left the company.

In the post-mortem, one of the steering committee members said what everyone had been thinking: "We all knew this was failing six months ago. Why didn't anyone say it?"

The answer was uncomfortable but clear: we'd all been conflict-averse. Raising the truth would have created tension, made the sponsor defensive, forced difficult conversations about accountability. So we'd stayed polite, stayed collegial, and let a recoverable problem become a catastrophic failure.

That's the cost of conflict avoidance: not peace, but deferred disaster.

Why Leaders Avoid Conflict

I have observed that consensus-seeking creates fragmentation and how clarity beats agreement. But beneath both patterns lies a deeper issue: most leaders are conflict-averse. We've been trained to see conflict as failure rather than as a tool.

The training starts early. In school, we're rewarded for getting along, for being team players, for not causing trouble. In our early careers, we learn that challenging authority is risky, that disagreeing with senior leaders can stall advancement, that being "difficult" gets you labeled as not a cultural fit.

By the time we reach leadership positions, conflict avoidance is so deeply ingrained that we don't even recognize we're doing it. We call it "being diplomatic," "building consensus," or "maintaining team harmony." We've convinced ourselves that avoiding conflict is a leadership virtue.

It's not. It's a leadership failure.

I learned this through painful experience. I'd spent years believing that my job as a leader was to minimize friction, smooth over disagreements, and keep everyone happy. I thought conflict meant I'd failed to create the right culture.

Then I started noticing a pattern: the teams that looked the most harmonious on the surface were often the ones making the worst decisions. Meanwhile, teams that argued openly—sometimes uncomfortably—were consistently making better calls.

The high-harmony teams had learned to avoid disagreement. They'd nod along in meetings even when they had concerns. They'd express doubts privately after meetings rather than during them. They'd let decisions proceed unchallenged to avoid the discomfort of conflict.

The result? Bad ideas went forward because nobody was willing to challenge them. Problems festered because nobody wanted to surface them. Mediocre work was accepted because pointing out quality issues felt too confrontational.

The teams that argued, by contrast, had developed a different skill: they'd learned to separate disagreement from disrespect. They could challenge each other's ideas vigorously while maintaining relationships. They didn't avoid conflict—they channeled it productively.

When Conflict Avoidance Costs You Everything

The steering committee failure was one example. But the pattern repeated across my career in ways both large and small.

An engineering team avoided a hard conversation about architectural decisions. They knew the proposed approach had scalability issues, but raising concerns felt like questioning the tech lead's expertise. Six months later, they hit the scaling wall. The rework cost four times what it would have cost to address the issue early.

The team didn't lack technical knowledge. They lacked the willingness to have productive conflict when it mattered.

In another case, an executive team avoided addressing a performance issue with a peer. Everyone knew the sales leader wasn't delivering, but he'd been with the company for fifteen years and was well-liked. Raising performance concerns felt harsh, disloyal, like betraying a friend.

So they waited. They hoped it would improve. They made excuses.

Chapter 7
Conflict as a Competitive Advantage

Two years later, the sales organization was in crisis. The leader finally left, but the damage was done—lost deals, demoralized team, broken processes. The cost of avoiding one difficult conversation was two years of organizational dysfunction.

I've seen this pattern in hiring decisions, strategic choices, partnership agreements, and client relationships. In every case, the dynamic was the same: people had concerns, but voicing them felt uncomfortable, so they stayed quiet. And staying quiet always—always—made the problem worse.

The Paradox of Psychological Safety

Here's what confused me for years: I'd read that psychological safety was essential for high-performing teams. But I'd also observed that the most psychologically 'safe' environments, places where nobody ever felt uncomfortable, were often mediocre.

The resolution came when I finally understood what psychological safety actually means.

As Edmondson's research showed, high-performing teams don't avoid conflict, they handle it productively.

Psychological safety enables disagreement without fear.

Psychological safety doesn't mean comfort. It means you can take interpersonal risks, including voicing disagreement, admitting mistakes, or challenging assumptions, without fear of punishment or humiliation.

The highest-performing teams I've observed are not the most comfortable. They're the ones where conflict happens early, openly, and productively. Where people challenge each other's thinking without it becoming

143

personal. Where disagreement is welcomed as a tool for better decisions, not avoided as a threat to harmony.

The lowest-performing teams feel "safe" in the wrong way: safe from challenge, safe from accountability, safe from having to defend their ideas. That's not psychological safety—that's psychological complacency.

Real psychological safety enables hard conversations, not comfortable ones.

Constructive Confrontation

Andy Grove at Intel built a culture of "constructive confrontation", Intel's version of what Amazon later called "disagree and commit". Leaders challenged each other's ideas directly, debated vigorously, disagreed openly. But once decisions were made, disagreement ceased and execution began.

This wasn't about being combative, it was about separating decision-quality from ego.

I watched this principle transform a leadership team I was coaching. They'd been operating in what I'd call 'harmony mode,' polite, collegial, and careful not to step on anyone's toes. Decisions took weeks because nobody wanted to push back. Quality suffered because critique felt like personal attack.

We introduced one rule: in strategy discussions, at least three people must voice substantive disagreement before we move forward. Not token objections, genuine challenges to the logic, assumptions, or approach.

The first few meetings were awkward. People didn't know how to disagree without it feeling personal. We had to coach them: "Challenge the idea, not the person. Say 'I see a risk with this approach' not 'You're wrong.'"

But after a month, something shifted. People started challenging each other more freely. Debates got sharper. Ideas got stress-tested before decisions, not after. Decision quality improved dramatically because bad ideas were caught early through productive conflict rather than discovered late through expensive failure.

Six months later, one team member said: "I used to think conflict meant something was broken. Now I realize absence of conflict means we're not thinking hard enough."

Tharkam: The Ancient Art of Principled Opposition

The breakthrough in my understanding of productive conflict came from an unexpected source: an ancient Indian philosophical tradition called Tharkam.

I encountered it during a consulting engagement in India. An executive I was coaching described how they'd been trained in the practice of intellectual debate, not to win arguments, but to strengthen thinking through rigorous challenge.

Tharkam has ancient roots in Indian philosophical traditions, particularly the Nyaya school of logic and "shastrartha" debates. These weren't casual discussions but rigorous, structured challenges designed to expose logical flaws and weak premises.

The goal wasn't winning, it was arriving at truth through the collision of ideas. Both participants emerged with sharper thinking, regardless of outcome. The tradition valued intellectual honesty, logical rigor, and willingness to abandon weak positions.

What fascinated me was how different this was from Western debate traditions, where the goal is often to "win" by persuading an audience. In Tharkam, there's no audience to persuade. Both participants are seeking truth, and both benefit when flaws are exposed.

The executive described how his team used this approach in strategy sessions. One person would propose an approach. Another would be assigned the role of 'principled opposition,' with the job of finding every logical flaw, weak assumption, and gap in reasoning.

Critically, being assigned principled opposition wasn't personal. It was a role, rotated across team members. You'd argue against a proposal one week, then watch someone else argue against yours the next week. This separated ego from inquiry.

The results were remarkable. Bad strategies were caught early. Good strategies got stronger through the stress-testing. And nobody felt personally attacked because challenge was part of the process, not a sign of disrespect.

I started introducing Tharkam-inspired practices into my own teams. In strategic planning sessions, I'd assign someone to play "red team", their explicit job was to find holes in our thinking. In budget reviews, I'd ask someone to argue why we shouldn't approve a proposal, even if they personally supported it.

At first, people struggled with the artificiality. But over time, it normalized productive opposition. Challenge became expected, even welcomed. And the quality of our decisions improved because we were stress-testing ideas before committing to them, not defending them after failure.

Chapter 7
Conflict as a Competitive Advantage

The Conflict Spectrum

Harmful Avoidance	Artificial Harmony	Productive Conflict	Destructive conflict	Toxic Fighting
Suppressed disagreement	Polite disagreement	Open challenge of ideas	Personal attacks	Constant hostility
Let Problems Fester	Concerns raised gently	Vigorous debate	Ego-driven arguments	No psychological safety
Comfort over Truth	Challenge feels risky	Separate ideas from ego	Win at all costs	Pure dysfunction
Outcome				
Bad decisions, Delayed Problems	Result: Mediocre decisions, slow response	Better decisions, fast problem solving	Damaged relationships, poor execution	Organizational failure

Most teams default to artificial harmony (center-left). High performers operate in productive conflict (center). The goal isn't to avoid conflict—it's to practice it productively

Most teams default to artificial harmony (center-left). High performers operate in productive conflict (center). The goal isn't to avoid conflict— it's to practice it productively.

The Five Types of Conflict

Not all conflict is created equal. Understanding which type you're dealing with helps you navigate it effectively.

Task conflict: What should we do? This is conflict about goals, strategies, or priorities. It's the most productive type when handled well. Example: "Should we prioritize market expansion or product deepening?"

Task conflict is productive when it's focused on outcomes and backed by evidence. It becomes destructive when people get attached to their position rather than finding the best answer.

Process conflict: How should we do it? This is conflict about methods, workflows, or approaches. Example: "Should we use agile or waterfall methodology?"

Process conflict can be productive in the design phase but destructive during execution. Once you've committed to an approach, relitigating process wastes energy.

Relationship conflict: Personal dynamics. This is conflict that's fundamentally about interpersonal friction—personality clashes, communication styles, trust issues.

Relationship conflict is almost never productive. It creates emotional residue that undermines even good task conflict. This is the type to minimize or address directly through mediation.

Status conflict: Who gets credit or authority? This is conflict about recognition, control, or hierarchy. Example: Two leaders both claiming ownership of a successful initiative.

Status conflict is toxic. It makes everything personal and ego-driven. The antidote is making outcomes matter more than credit, and focusing on organizational success rather than individual recognition.

Values conflict: Fundamental principles. This is conflict about core beliefs or ethical boundaries. Example: "Should we pursue this lucrative opportunity if it conflicts with our stated values?"

Values conflict is the hardest to resolve because it's not about data—it's about identity. Sometimes it can't be resolved, only managed through clarity about which values take precedence in different contexts.

Ground Rules for Productive Conflict

Over years of practice, I developed ground rules that transformed how teams handled disagreement:

1. Separate ideas from identity. Attack reasoning, not people. "This approach has risks" not "You're being naive." Language matters. Frame disagreement as exploring the idea, not judging the person.

2. Be specific. "The timeline feels aggressive" is vague. "We're assuming 2-week sprints but we've never delivered better than 3-week sprints on similar complexity" is useful. Specificity lets you debate facts rather than feelings.

3. Question before concluding. Understand their logic before challenging it. "Help me understand why you think X will work..." before "I disagree because..." You might discover your disagreement was based on misunderstanding their actual position.

4. Acknowledge merit publicly. "That's a good point" costs nothing and makes disagreement less personal. Even when you ultimately disagree, acknowledging strong elements of their argument maintains respect.

5. Make it about outcomes. "What's best for the customer?" not "Who's right?" Reframe conflict around shared goals. This depersonalizes disagreement and focuses on solving the right problem.

6. Disagree early, commit after. : Voice disagreement during decisions, commit fully during execution. Conflict at the right time, not after.

When Conflict Works—and When It Doesn't

I'd be dishonest if I claimed productive conflict always works. Through trial and error, I learned when to lean into conflict and when to handle it differently.

Conflict works when:

Stakes are high and decisions are complex. The bigger the decision, the more you need vigorous debate to stress-test thinking. Acquisitions, strategy shifts, major investments, these benefit from structured opposition.

You have time to work through it. Good conflict takes time. If you need a decision in the next hour, debate might not be the right approach. But for important non-urgent decisions, invest the time.

Psychological safety exists. People need to trust that disagreement won't be punished. If people fear speaking up, conflict won't be productive, it'll just drive concerns underground.

People share fundamental goals. Conflict is productive when you disagree on approach but agree on the desired outcome. When people have different goals, "debate" becomes political maneuvering.

Conflict fails when:

It becomes personal. Once conflict shifts from ideas to attacks on character or competence, it's no longer productive. It's just destructive.

People aren't listening. If participants are just waiting for their turn to talk, repeating positions without engaging with others' points, you're not having productive conflict—you're having parallel monologues.

Chapter 7
Conflict as a Competitive Advantage

Stakes are too low. Not every decision needs vigorous debate. Save conflict for things that matter. Otherwise you exhaust people and create a culture where everything becomes a battle.

Power dynamics are unequal. When a junior person "disagrees" with a senior executive, psychological safety matters enormously. If the junior person feels their career is at risk, conflict won't be honest.

Building a Conflict-Capable Culture

Individual practices matter, but culture change requires organizational commitment.

Here's what building a conflict-capable culture looked like in practice:

We normalized principled opposition. In strategy sessions, we rotated "red team" assignments. Being asked to challenge a proposal wasn't criticism, it was a valued contribution to better thinking.

We made conflict visible and safe. When good conflict happened, we acknowledged it: "That debate was exactly what we needed. Thank you both for pushing each other's thinking."

We separated debate from decisions. We had explicit phases: first debate vigorously, then the DRI decides, then we commit. This gave people permission to argue during debate without feeling they were undermining decisions.

We addressed bad conflict directly. When conflict became personal, we intervened immediately, not to shut down disagreement, but to redirect it back to ideas and outcomes.

We celebrated mind-changing. When someone changed their position based on debate, we recognized it publicly: "It takes intellectual honesty to update your thinking. That's what we want to see more of."

We measured it. In retrospectives, we asked: Did anyone hold back a concern? Did debate happen during decisions or after? Did anyone feel personally attacked? The data helped us course-correct.

The cultural shift took time. People needed to see that disagreement truly was valued, not just tolerated. They needed to experience challenge that improved decisions without damaging relationships. They needed proof that principled opposition was rewarded, not punished.

But once it took hold, the change was dramatic. Decision quality improved. Problems surfaced earlier. Execution was faster because we'd worked through concerns upfront rather than discovering them during implementation.

The Conversation I Finally Had

Five years after that steering committee failure, I faced a similar situation, but handled it completely differently.

We were reviewing a major product launch that wasn't meeting targets. The product lead gave an optimistic update about how we were "gaining traction" and "seeing positive early indicators."

But the data told a different story. Customer acquisition was below target. Retention was concerning. The product-market fit wasn't there.

This time, I didn't stay silent.

"I'm going to push back on the framing," I said. "The data doesn't support optimism. We're not gaining traction, we're failing to get traction. I think we need to have a hard conversation about whether this product has a viable path forward."

The room tensed. The product lead looked defensive. But I'd learned how to frame conflict productively.

Chapter 7
Conflict as a Competitive Advantage

"You've put enormous effort into this," I continued. "The execution has been solid. But effort doesn't guarantee market success. I respect everything you've done, and I want to have an honest conversation about what the data is telling us, separate from how much we've invested."

What followed was an uncomfortable but necessary debate. The product lead defended the vision. Others voiced concerns they'd been holding back. We examined the data without spin. We discussed pivot options versus sunset options.

By the end of the meeting, we'd made a hard call: pivot the product dramatically or wind it down within 90 days based on clear success metrics.

It was uncomfortable. But it was productive. And it happened six months earlier than it would have if we'd kept avoiding the truth.

Three months later, the pivot worked. The repositioned product found traction. But even if it hadn't, we'd have made the wind-down decision rationally rather than letting it become a crisis.

That's what productive conflict enables: hard conversations when they're still productive, not after they become disasters.

Actions for Readers: Building Your Conflict Capability

Productive conflict is a skill, not a personality trait. Here's how to develop it:

The Conflict Audit:

Think about your last three difficult conversations you avoided. For each:

- What was the real issue you didn't address?
- What was the cost of avoidance?

- What would productive conflict have looked like?

If you can't identify three avoided conflicts, you're either in an unusually healthy environment or (more likely) you're not noticing the patterns.

This Week - Start Small:

Day 1-2: Name one thing that needs to be said. What's the conversation you've been avoiding? Write down exactly what needs to be addressed. Specifics, not generalities.

Day 3-4: Practice the opening. "I need to raise something that's been bothering me..." Draft the first two sentences. Make them specific, not accusatory.

Day 5: Have the conversation. Pick the smallest, lowest-stakes version. Practice productive conflict on something that matters but won't explode if you're clumsy.

This Month - Build the Muscle:

Install one Tharkam practice: In your next strategy discussion, assign someone to play "principled opposition"—their job is to challenge assumptions. Make it a role, not a personality conflict.

Try the "disagree" note: In your next meeting where you disagree but stay quiet, write down: "If I were being brave, I'd say..." Then decide: Is it worth saying? If yes, say it. If no, why not?

Establish conflict ground rules: With your team, agree on how you'll handle disagreement. Post them visibly. Reference them when conflict emerges.

This Quarter - Build the Culture:

Measure conflict quality:

- Track: How often do people voice disagreement in meetings?
- Track: How often do you discover after meetings that people disagreed but stayed silent?
- Track: How quickly do conflicts get raised vs. how long they fester?

Celebrate good conflict:

- When someone raises a hard truth, thank them publicly
- When someone changes their mind based on debate, recognize intellectual honesty
- When conflict leads to better decisions, connect the dots explicitly

Practice Tharkam:

- Monthly "red team" sessions where the goal is to find holes in current strategy
- Assign rotating "opposition" roles in planning meetings
- Reward finding flaws early, not hiding them until they become crises

A Closing Reflection

That steering committee meeting taught me something I should have learned earlier: the most expensive thing you can do is avoid difficult conversations.

Every time we stay silent to avoid discomfort, we trade short-term comfort for long-term cost. Every time we let a bad idea proceed unchallenged because debate feels uncomfortable, we're choosing failure over friction.

The organizations that win aren't the most harmonious. They're the ones that have learned to channel conflict productively, to debate vigorously during decisions, commit fully during execution, and separate disagreement from disrespect.

Conflict isn't a sign that something's broken. Often, it's a sign that people care enough to fight for what they think is right.

The question isn't whether you'll have conflict. The question is whether you'll use it as a competitive advantage or let it become an organizational liability.

Ten years ago, I would have done anything to avoid the kind of direct challenge I gave that product lead. I'd have stayed silent, hoped things improved, and watched failure unfold gradually.

Now I understand: the kindest thing I can do as a leader isn't to make people comfortable. It's to create an environment where truth gets spoken early, ideas get challenged rigorously, and conflict happens productively before it becomes crisis.

That's not just better leadership. It's the only way to build organizations capable of making hard decisions fast, learning from debate, and adapting before problems become disasters.

The next time you're in a meeting where everyone's nodding but nobody's challenging, remember: silence isn't harmony. It's often just deferred conflict.

And deferred conflict always costs more.

Chapter 8
Ownership That Scales

"So technically, your building is 25 meters outside my jurisdiction."

The Empowerment That Wasn't

The transformation initiative had everything needed: sponsorship, budget, timeline, talented project manager.

On paper, the role was 'empowered.' The word appeared everywhere: kick-off emails, charters, executive speeches. 'You're empowered to make the decisions necessary for success.

Six months in, momentum was gone. Decisions kept escalating. Problems were surfaced, solutions proposed, and then nothing happened for weeks. When approvals finally came, the situation had already shifted.

I watched this in a steering committee meeting. The person presented three options for addressing a technical roadblock. The sponsor asked questions, nodded thoughtfully, then said: "Let me think about it and get back to you."

After the meeting, I asked the person in the role, 'You're supposed to be empowered. Why didn't you just decide?

There was a pause, then the response came. 'The first time I decided without checking, I was called into the office and told I should have consulted first. I'm not empowered. I'm just responsible if things go wrong.

That's fake empowerment: the responsibility without the authority. The accountability without the autonomy. The ownership that's really just a blame waiting to happen.

I'd seen this pattern countless times. Leaders who said "you're empowered" but maintained approval chains for everything. Organizations that talked about ownership but punished independent decisions. Teams given responsibility for outcomes they had no real control over.

We'd confused delegation with empowerment. We'd mistaken assigning work for building ownership.

Chapter 8
Ownership That Scales

Real ownership, the kind that actually scales, requires something fundamentally different.

From Responsibility to Ownership

In Chapter 4, I described how real authority comes from taking responsibility beyond your job description. This chapter is about systematizing that principle, how to build organizations where ownership scales beyond individual heroes.

The distinction between responsibility and ownership matters more than most leaders realize.

Responsibility is about tasks and compliance. You're responsible for completing your assigned work, following processes, meeting deadlines. Responsibility is transactional: you do what you're told, you get paid.

Ownership is about outcomes and judgment. You own a result, not just a task. You have authority to make decisions, not just execute instructions. You're accountable for whether it works, not just whether you did your part.

I learned this distinction watching two product managers operate completely differently.

The first managed by responsibility. When asked about a delayed feature, he'd explain which teams hadn't delivered their pieces on time. "I did my part. I wrote the specs, scheduled the meetings, tracked the milestones. But engineering was late, design missed deadlines, and testing found issues." Technically accurate. Completely missing the point.

The second managed by ownership. When a feature was delayed, he'd say: "We're behind schedule. Here's what I'm doing about it: reprioritizing with engineering to unblock them, simplifying the design to reduce complexity, and adding test coverage earlier to catch issues faster." Same delay, completely different response. He owned the outcome, not just his task.

The difference wasn't personality, it was how they understood their role. The first saw himself as a coordinator of other people's work. The second saw himself as the owner of a customer outcome.

The DRI Foundation

I introduced the idea of a Directly Responsible Individual earlier as a practical tool. Here, it matters as something deeper: a foundation for ownership at scale. The DRI (Directly Responsible Individual) concept is foundational to ownership at scale: one person owns the outcome, gathers input, decides, and delivers. When everyone is accountable, nobody is. When one person is the DRI, ownership is clear.

But making DRIs actually work requires more than just naming someone. It requires genuine empowerment—not the lip-service kind I described elsewhere where you say "you're empowered" while maintaining approval chains. Real empowerment means accepting that people will make different choices than you would, and being okay with that.

The transformation came when we moved from assigning DRIs to actually empowering them.

We gave DRIs three things they'd rarely had before:

Decision authority within boundaries. Not "check with me before deciding" but "here are the constraints, here's the outcome we need, you decide how to get there."

Resource control. Not "request budget through me" but "here's your budget allocation, you allocate it based on your judgment."

Outcome accountability. Not "complete these tasks" but "deliver this result by this date, measure success this way."

The shift was uncomfortable. Leaders had to let go of control. DRIs had to step into genuine accountability. Both sides had to trust the system.

But once it took hold, the impact was immediate. Decision speed increased because people weren't waiting for approval. Quality improved because owners felt genuine accountability, not just task completion. Innovation accelerated because people had authority to experiment.

The Five Levels of Ownership

Not all ownership is created equal. Through years of observing what works and what doesn't, I identified five levels of ownership maturity:

Level 1: No ownership (pure execution). You're told what to do, how to do it, when it's due. You execute instructions. If something goes wrong, it's not your problem, you did what you were told. Most entry-level roles operate here by design.

Level 2: Partial ownership (do the task, escalate problems). You own completing your assigned work, but when problems emerge, you escalate. "I can't finish this because X is blocking me." You identify issues but don't solve them. Many mid-level roles get stuck here.

Level 3: Problem-solving ownership (identify and solve within scope). You don't just flag problems, you solve them within your domain. "X was blocking me, so I found a workaround." You're proactive, but still constrained to your defined area. This is where most strong individual contributors operate.

Level 4: Outcome ownership (own the result, not just tasks). You own whether the customer problem gets solved, not just whether you completed your part. If something's broken and it affects your outcome, you fix it, even if it's "not your job." This is where effective leaders operate.

Level 5: Strategic ownership (shape direction, not just deliver). You don't just execute strategy—you shape it. You see opportunities and problems before they're obvious. You make bets, take calculated risks, and own the consequences. This is where transformative leaders operate.

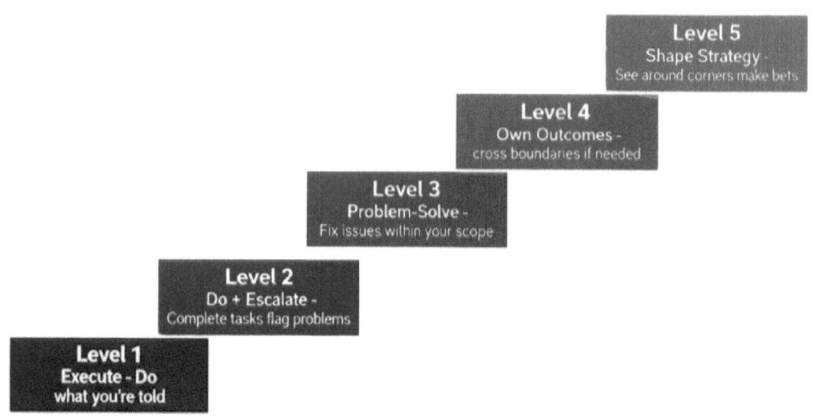

The goal isn't to have everyone at Level 5—that's neither realistic nor necessary. But understanding these levels helps you match people to roles, identify growth opportunities, and diagnose why ownership isn't working.

Working Backwards from the Outcome

One practice transformed how we built ownership: Amazon's "working backwards" process.

Instead of starting with what you can do and seeing where it leads, start with the outcome you want and work backward to what needs to happen.

Amazon famously writes the press release before building the product. Not as PR—as clarification. If you can't write a compelling announcement of success, you probably don't understand what success looks like.

We adapted this for our context. For any major initiative, the DRI writes the "success story" first:

What will we celebrate when this is done? Not activities completed, but outcomes achieved. "Customers can now..." or "The business can now..."

What will customers/stakeholders say about it? Specific quotes capturing the value delivered.

What metrics will prove it worked? Concrete, measurable outcomes that show impact.

What was hard about this? The challenges we overcame to make it happen.

Only after writing the success story do we plan backward: What needs to be true for this outcome? What must we build, change, or solve? What's the sequence of milestones?

This practice does three things:

Forces clarity. If you can't describe success compellingly, you don't understand what you're building. Many initiatives fail not because of execution, because nobody really knew what success looked like.

Creates ownership. Writing the success story makes the outcome real. You're not just completing tasks, you're delivering something specific that matters.

Enables autonomy. When outcomes are crystal clear, the path to get there can be flexible. You don't need constant oversight when everyone knows what winning looks like.

I watched this work powerfully on a customer experience initiative. The DRI's success story started: "Customers tell us they love doing business with us because we resolve issues on first contact, not after multiple frustrating interactions."

That one sentence—"resolve on first contact"—clarified everything. It meant we couldn't just "improve response times" or "increase satisfaction scores." We had to fundamentally redesign how support worked. The clarity enabled the DRI to make bold decisions about process changes, tool investments, and organizational structure without constant approval because the outcome was unambiguous.

The Ownership Killers

I learned what enables ownership by watching what kills it. Five patterns consistently destroy ownership culture:

1. Unclear decision rights. "You own it but need approval for everything." This is the most common killer. People are told they're accountable but discover they can't actually decide anything meaningful. Every choice requires escalation. Ownership becomes a title without substance.

Fix: Define explicitly what decisions the owner can make without escalation. Use two-door framework: reversible decisions? They decide. Irreversible? Escalate. Create clarity, not theater.

2. Responsibility without resources. Accountable for outcomes but no authority over budget, people, or priorities. You're blamed when results don't materialize but have no real control over the levers that produce results.

Fix: Authority must match accountability. If someone owns an outcome, they need control over the inputs, budget allocation, resource decisions, priority calls. Otherwise you're setting them up to fail.

3. Micromanagement. "You own it... but do it exactly my way." Leaders who can't resist telling people how to work destroy ownership. The message is clear: your judgment doesn't matter, just follow my instructions.

Fix: Define the outcome and boundaries, then step back. Judge results, not methods. If someone achieves the outcome differently than you would have, that's success, not a problem.

4. Blame culture. Mistakes are punished, so people avoid decisions that carry risk. They escalate everything, follow rules rigidly, and protect themselves from accountability rather than embracing it.

Fix: Separate learning from consequences. Bad outcomes from reasonable decisions are learning opportunities. Bad outcomes from negligence or repeated mistakes have consequences. Make the distinction explicit.

5. Hero culture. Rewards go to people who personally save the day, not to those who build systems that prevent fires. This encourages hoarding ownership rather than scaling it.

Fix: Celebrate system building, not heroics. Recognize people whose teams deliver without them. Reward leaders who develop other owners.

When Ownership Goes Wrong

I've watched ownership initiatives fail spectacularly. The patterns are instructive:

A manager I'll call Ravi struggled to let go. Intellectually, he understood that ownership meant giving his team decision authority. But emotionally, he couldn't handle it. Every time his team made a choice he disagreed with, even when it worked, he second-guessed them publicly. Within three months, they'd stopped making decisions entirely. They'd learned that "ownership" meant blame when things went wrong and criticism when Ravi disagreed with their approach.

The problem wasn't the team, it was Ravi's inability to genuinely empower them. Ownership without trust is just performance.

On the flip side, I watched a team member I'll call Rekha struggle to step into ownership. She'd spent her career in organizations where taking initiative was punished, where making decisions without permission was career suicide. When we gave her genuine ownership of a product area, she kept asking for approval. "Can I prioritize feature X?" Yes, that's your call. "Should I hire this candidate?" Your team, your decision. "Is it okay if I delay the release by a week?" You own the outcome, you make that call.

It took six months of coaching, and seeing that decisions would not be second-guessed, before real ownership took hold. The pattern was so ingrained that permission-seeking felt safer than deciding.

Both stories illustrate the same truth: ownership is a cultural muscle, not a structural change. You can't just declare "everyone now has ownership" and expect it to work. People need time to develop comfort with genuine authority, and leaders need to genuinely let go.

Building Ownership Culture

Individual practices matter, but cultural transformation requires systematic commitment. Here's what building ownership culture looked like:

Model letting go publicly. I started announcing when I was stepping back from decisions. "This is Sarah's call now. I trust her judgment. I won't override unless she asks for input." Making my letting-go visible gave others permission to do the same.

Address fake empowerment immediately. When leaders said people were empowered but then overrode their decisions, I called it out directly: "You just undermined the ownership you said you were giving them. Either they own it or you do. Pick one."

Create consequences for decision-avoidance. When people escalated decisions they should own, we'd respond: "That's your decision to make. What do you think we should do?" Pushing back on escalations trained people to own their domain.

Celebrate ownership broadly. When someone made a tough call without escalating, solved a cross-functional problem, or delivered an outcome their way rather than following the "standard" approach, we recognized it publicly. Culture shifts when you celebrate what you want to see more of.

The Transformation That Lasted

Five years after we started systematically building ownership culture, I visited a team facing a major client crisis. The client's implementation was failing, threatening a multi-million-dollar relationship.

In our old culture, this would have escalated immediately to senior leadership. We'd have assembled a crisis team, held daily war room meetings, and micromanaged every detail until it was resolved.

Instead, the product DRI assembled her cross-functional team, diagnosed root cause, developed a recovery plan, and executed it—all within 72 hours. She kept leadership informed but didn't ask for permission or wait for direction.

When she presented the resolution to the executive team afterward, the CEO asked: "How did you have authority to commit those resources without escalation?"

"Because I own this product outcome," she said. "That includes handling crises. I stayed within my budget allocation and decision rights. The client's stable now."

The CEO looked at me. "This would have taken us two weeks and five executive meetings before."

"Exactly," I said. "That's what ownership at scale looks like."

That's when I knew the transformation had stuck. Ownership wasn't a program or an initiative. It had become how we worked. People understood their domains, had authority to act, and felt genuine accountability for outcomes.

The structure had finally caught up to the aspiration.

Actions for Readers: Building Ownership at Scale

Examine your team's current ownership reality. For each of your direct reports:

- Do they have a clear DRI area where they own outcomes (not just tasks)?
- Can they make meaningful decisions without your approval?
- When was the last time they solved a significant problem without escalating to you?

If most answers are unclear or "never," you've built dependency, not ownership.

This Week - Test Real Empowerment:

Monday: Identify one decision you typically make. Give it completely to someone else—not just the work, the actual decision. Tell them the outcome you need and the boundaries, then step back.

Tuesday-Thursday: Resist the urge to check in or "help." Let them own it. Notice your own discomfort—that's the cost of genuine empowerment.

Friday: Debrief. How did they handle it? What did you learn about your ability to let go? What did they learn about ownership?

This Month - Install Ownership Infrastructure:

Define clear DRI areas for each team member:

- What outcome do they own (not task, outcome)?
- What decisions can they make without escalation?
- What resources/authority do they have?
- How will success be measured?

Create the "Working Backwards" practice:

- For the next major initiative, write the success announcement first
- What will you celebrate when it's done?
- Work backward from that to what needs to happen
- Assign one DRI for the entire journey

Identify ownership killers in your current practices:

- Where do you require approval for things people should own?
- Where is responsibility clear but authority missing?
- Where do you inadvertently rescue people from consequences?

This Quarter - Transform the Culture:

Make ownership visible:

- Create a public DRI map showing who owns what outcomes
- In every meeting discussing an initiative, answer: "Who's the DRI?"

- If there's no clear answer, the meeting ends until someone is assigned

Celebrate ownership publicly:

- When someone makes a tough call without escalating, recognize it
- When someone owns a mistake and fixes it, highlight the ownership (not the mistake)
- When someone achieves an outcome their way (not your way), acknowledge their approach worked

Practice letting go:

- Identify one area where you're the bottleneck
- Find someone capable of owning it
- Give them outcome clarity and boundaries
- Step back for 30 days
- Measure: Did it work? What did you both learn?

Address fake empowerment:

- If you say people are empowered, audit whether they actually are
- Count how many times you override decisions "empowered" people make
- If it's more than rarely, you have a trust problem, not an empowerment structure

A Closing Reflection

That project manager who wasn't really empowered taught me something fundamental: the gap between what leaders say and what organizations actually do is where ownership dies.

Chapter 8
Ownership That Scales

We say "you're empowered" but maintain approval chains. We say "you own it" but second-guess every decision. We say "take initiative" but punish mistakes. We say "be accountable" but don't give authority.

The words are easy. The reality is hard. Because real ownership requires leaders to genuinely let go, not just delegate tasks, but surrender control over how outcomes get achieved.

That surrender is uncomfortable. It means accepting that people will make different choices than you would. It means living with decisions you disagree with. It means trusting that when mistakes happen, people will own them and learn.

But it's the only path to scale. You can't build organizations that grow beyond you while maintaining control over everything. At some point, you have to choose: maintain control or build owners. You can't do both.

Ten years ago, I would have responded to that client crisis by assembling my own war room, pulling together resources, and personally driving the resolution. I'd have been the hero. I'd have saved the day.

Now I understand: the real victory wasn't that the crisis got resolved. It's that it got resolved without me. Because the DRI had genuine ownership, the authority to act, the resources to execute, and the accountability that makes both meaningful.

That's what ownership at scale looks like. Not everyone waiting for you to decide. Everyone capable of deciding within their domain, while you focus on the decisions only you can make.

The question isn't whether you can build an organization of owners. The question is whether you're willing to stop being the owner of everything.

That's the shift that makes everything else possible.

Chapter 9
Decisions at Speed

"MANAGEMENT WANTS US TO TAKE DECISIONS WITH SPEED."

The Launch That Wasn't

The product was ready. Engineering had completed development. Design had finalized the interface. Marketing had prepared the launch campaign. Sales had trained on the new offering.

We were ready to launch. Except we weren't launching.

Instead, we were scheduling another review meeting. The third in as many weeks. Not because anyone had identified new issues, because the executive team wanted "one more look."

At the review meeting, executives asked the same questions answered in previous meetings. Requested the same analyses already completed. Raised the same concerns already addressed.

After ninety minutes, the decision: "Let's reconvene next week after we've had more time to review the materials."

I watched the product lead's face. The team had been ready to launch six weeks earlier. Now the work had shifted to managing executive anxiety instead of serving customers.

By the time we finally approved the launch, two competitors had already released similar products. Our window had narrowed. What should have been a market-leading move became a catch-up play.

The product didn't fail because it was wrong. It failed because we were slow. And we were slow not because we lacked information—because we lacked the courage to decide.

When Speed Becomes Strategy

Earlier in the book, I described how consensus creates comfort but kills clarity. This chapter is about the related problem: how consensus kills speed, and what to do about it.

Speed isn't just operational efficiency. It's strategic advantage. In fast-moving markets, the team that decides and moves fastest often wins—not because their decisions are better, but because they learn and adapt faster.

Amazon doesn't dominate because they make perfect decisions. They dominate because they make fast decisions, learn from them quickly, and iterate. Netflix doesn't lead because they never make mistakes. They lead because they experiment rapidly and kill what doesn't work before competitors even launch.

The organizations I've watched struggle aren't slow because they lack talent or resources. They're slow because their decision-making processes optimize for comfort over speed, consensus over clarity, perfection over learning.

Every layer of approval adds days or weeks. Every stakeholder who must be consulted extends timelines. Every requirement for unanimous agreement creates veto points where decisions stall.

The result: organizations that move at the pace of their slowest decision-maker, which is almost always too slow.

The Two-Door Framework

Jeff Bezos describes this through the two-door decision framework. Irreversible decisions, or one-way doors, require deliberation because once made, they are hard to undo. Reversible decisions, or two-way doors, should be made quickly by the people closest to the context. The leadership task is to distinguish between the two, empower teams to move fast where decisions can be reversed, and slow down deliberately where they cannot. The mistake most organizations make is assuming far more decisions are irreversible than they actually are.

This kills speed.

I watched this play out with a vendor selection. The team needed to choose between two software platforms. Neither was a permanent commitment, both had contract exit clauses, migration was feasible, the stakes were modest.

But the decision process treated it like we were choosing a spouse. Months of analysis. Endless stakeholder meetings. Detailed comparison matrices. Risk assessments for scenarios that would never materialize.

Four months in, I stopped the process: "If we choose wrong, what's the actual cost to reverse it?"

The answer: roughly two weeks of work and maybe $50,000 in switching costs.

"And the cost of delaying this decision another month?"

The answer: far more than $50,000 in delayed benefits, opportunity cost, and team frustration.

We made the decision in the next three days. Picked a vendor. Implemented. Learned. It worked fine. And if it hadn't, we would have switched.

That's the two-door principle in action: match decision speed to actual reversibility, not perceived importance.

Chapter 9
Decisions at Speed

Decision Speed Framework- Two door approach

Most decisions fall in the left column (reversible). Stop treating them like the right column. Speed comes from knowing the difference.

Speed Requires Clear Ownership

Speed requires clear ownership, the DRI principle is the key. When everyone can weigh in but one person decides, you get input without paralysis.

The vendor selection dragged because nobody owned the decision. IT thought the business units should decide. Business units thought IT should decide. Finance wanted input because of budget implications. Everyone had a voice, nobody had authority.

Once we named a DRI, gave them clear decision authority, defined the inputs they needed, set a decision deadline, the process accelerated immediately. Not because the DRI was smarter or had more information. Because accountability was clear.

Meeting Culture That Kills Speed

Beyond the meeting reforms I described in Chapters 1-2, decision speed requires one additional practice: clarity about who decides before the meeting starts.

If you can't name who's deciding before the meeting, you're not having a decision meeting, you're having a discussion meeting. Discussion has value, but don't confuse it with deciding.

The Six-Page Memo

One practice transformed our decision speed: Amazon's six-page memo replacing PowerPoint presentations.

Instead of slide decks, decision proposals are written as six-page narratives. Meetings start with everyone silently reading the memo for 20-30 minutes. Then discussion.

Why it works:

Writing forces clarity. You can't hide weak thinking in a narrative the way you can in bullet points. If the logic doesn't flow, the memo reveals it.

Reading creates shared context. Everyone starts the meeting with the same information, not fragmented understanding from skimming slides.

Discussion focuses on substance. No time wasted on "what did that slide mean?" Questions go straight to the actual issues.

Chapter 9
Decisions at Speed

We adapted this for major decisions. The DRI writes a decision memo answering:

- What's the decision?
- What's the recommendation and why?
- What alternatives were considered?
- What are the risks?
- What's the reversibility?

Meetings start with silent reading. Discussion follows. Decision happens in that meeting, not in follow-ups.

Decision quality improved and speed increased. The discipline of writing exposed weak proposals before meetings, not during them. Good proposals moved faster because logic was clear.

When Slow Decisions Cost Everything

The cost of slow decisions isn't always obvious, but it's always real.

A marketing team wanted to test a new campaign approach. The creative was ready. The budget was allocated. The timing was right.

But the approval chain was brutal: marketing director → CMO → CFO (for budget) → CEO (for brand risk). Each level took days or weeks. Questions were answered. Revisions made. More questions asked.

Six weeks later, approval finally came. By then, the market moment had passed. The campaign launched to mediocre results because timing was wrong.

Nobody made a bad decision. But the decision velocity was so slow that a good idea became a wasted opportunity.

That's the hidden cost of slow decisions: not wrong choices, but right choices made too late to matter.

Speed vs. Quality: The False Trade-off

The most common objection to fast decisions: "But we'll sacrifice quality!"

This assumes speed and quality are opposed. They're not.

Slow decisions aren't higher quality, they're just slower. Often, they're lower quality because:

Analysis paralysis sets in. More data doesn't always mean better decisions. At some point, additional analysis just creates illusion of certainty without improving judgment.

Context changes while you deliberate. The market shifts. Competitors move. The information you based your analysis on becomes stale. Your "careful" decision is based on outdated assumptions.

Decision fatigue accumulates. The longer a decision drags, the more exhausted everyone becomes. Eventually people just want it over with, so they agree to whatever ends the process. That's not quality—it's surrender.

Fast decisions, by contrast, allow fast learning. Launch quickly, gather real data, adjust based on actual results rather than predicted scenarios. This learning loop often produces better outcomes than extended deliberation based on speculation.

When Mike Ventling took over as Global CFO, he faced a fragmented finance function spread across more than 100 countries. Consolidation looked impossible — everyone had their own systems, people, and processes. Most leaders before him avoided big moves, reasoning that the data was incomplete and the politics too complex.

Mike made a different call. He decided not to wait for perfect facts or universal approval. He saw that the longer EY waited, the harder it would be to act. So, he trusted his judgment — a combination of intuition and strategic foresight — and moved to transform the global finance function.

It was a bold decision, one that required persuasion more than authority. He built a vision for a unified global finance organization, started with pilot countries, and gradually pulled the rest in. There were sceptics, but the direction was clear. Within a few years, EY had a far more connected, globalized finance structure — something few thought possible when he started.

That experience taught me something profound:

Speed doesn't mean recklessness. It means having the conviction to **move when waiting would cost you more than acting.**

Mike's decision was not made with perfect data — it was made with perfect intent. That's leadership courage at its finest.

A bias for action doesn't mean impulsiveness. It means recognizing that speed itself is a decision, not an outcome.

The goal isn't reckless speed. It's appropriate speed: slow for irreversible decisions, fast for reversible ones.

The Five Speed Killers

Through years of observing organizational decision-making, I've identified five patterns that consistently kill speed:

1. Analysis paralysis. "We need more data" becomes a permanent state. There's always one more analysis to run, one more scenario to model, one more stakeholder to survey. The standard for "enough information" keeps rising, ensuring it's never reached.

Fix: Set a decision deadline before starting analysis. Define upfront: "What data would change this decision?" If the answer is unclear, you don't have an information problem, you have a clarity problem.

2. Consensus requirement. Everyone must agree before anything moves. Each stakeholder has implicit veto power. Decisions drift toward lowest-common-denominator compromises that satisfy no one.

Fix: Replace consensus with DRI + input. One person decides after gathering input. Consensus is optional. Clarity is mandatory.

3. Approval chains. Multiple sign-offs for reversible decisions. Each level adds days or weeks. By the time approvals complete, the world has changed.

Fix: Use the two-door framework. Reversible decisions don't need approval chains, they need clear boundaries and fast execution. Save approvals for irreversible commitments.

4. Meeting culture without decision authority. Endless discussions without anyone empowered to decide. Meetings end with "we'll think about it" or "let's schedule a follow-up."

Fix: Every decision meeting must have a named decision-maker present. If they're not in the room, it's not a decision meeting.

5. Risk aversion disguised as prudence. "Let's be careful" becomes "let's delay indefinitely." Every risk gets magnified. Every worst-case scenario gets treated as likely. Caution becomes paralysis.

Fix: Explicitly weigh both risks: the risk of deciding wrong AND the risk of deciding too late. Often the latter is higher but gets ignored.

Chapter 9
Decisions at Speed

Building a Bias for Action

Speed doesn't happen by accident. It requires deliberate cultural choices.

We made speed visible. We tracked average decision cycle time by category and published it monthly. When times increased, we investigated why. Measurement created accountability.

We celebrated fast good decisions. When teams made reversible decisions quickly and learned from them, we recognized it publicly. When decisions got reversed because we learned they were wrong, we celebrated the learning, not the "failure."

We created decision deadlines. Every significant decision got a "decide by" date announced upfront. New information could shift the date, but there was always a deadline visible. This prevented drift.

We pushed decisions down. Whenever something came to senior leadership for approval, we asked: "Could someone closer to the work make this call?" If yes, we pushed it down with clear boundaries.

We practiced "disagree and commit" publicly. Netflix codified this in their culture memo: "We're a team, not a family, which means we're not afraid to make fast decisions and course-correct if needed. Adequate performance gets a generous severance. We're a pro team, not a kids' recreational team."

When leaders disagreed with decisions but committed fully to execution, we highlighted it. This normalized dissent during decisions while reinforcing commitment during execution.

The cultural shift took time. People needed to see that fast decisions were rewarded, not punished. They needed to experience that reversing a decision was learning, not failure. They needed proof that DRIs would be supported, not second-guessed.

But once it took hold, the acceleration was dramatic. Decisions that used to take months took weeks. Decisions that took weeks took days. Not because we became reckless, because we matched decision speed to actual risk.

When to Slow Down

Speed isn't always the answer. Some decisions deserve deliberation.

Slow down for irreversible decisions. Acquisitions, major platform choices, entering new markets, these deserve thorough analysis. The cost of getting them wrong is high, and you can't easily reverse course.

Slow down when emotions are high. In crisis or conflict, initial reactions are often poor. Taking time to let emotions settle produces better judgment.

Slow down when expert input is needed. Some decisions require specialized knowledge. Rushing before expertise is gathered leads to uninformed choices.

Slow down when the team isn't aligned on the problem. If people are solving different problems, fast decisions just create confusion. Slow down enough to agree on what you're actually deciding.

But here's the key: these are specific exceptions, not general rules. Most decisions are reversible, not emotional, don't require specialized expertise, and the problem is clear. For those, which make up the vast majority, speed is strategic.

A Closing Story

Five years after our decision speed transformation, I observed a moment that showed how far we'd come.

Chapter 9
Decisions at Speed

A team faced a significant client issue. The client's implementation was failing. The product wasn't meeting their needs. The relationship was at risk.

In our old culture, this would have triggered weeks of analysis. Executive escalation. Multiple meetings to debate options. Careful consensus-building before acting.

Instead, the product DRI called a two-hour working session. The cross-functional pod diagnosed the issue, developed three options, evaluated them against clear criteria, and made the call to offer the client a significantly revised implementation approach with additional support resources. The decision was communicated to the client that afternoon. Implementation started the next day, and within two weeks the client was back on track.

Total time from problem identification to decision to action: less than 24 hours.

When she briefed leadership afterward, the CEO asked: "Did you have authority to commit those resources without escalation?"

"Yes," came the response. "Within my budget allocation and decision rights. The choice was between losing the client or investing in recovery. Recovery was clearly the right call."

"In the old culture," the CEO said, "this would have taken us three weeks of meetings and might have cost us the client. Now it took one day and saved the relationship."

That's what speed looks like when it's systematic, not heroic. When it's enabled by clear ownership, decision rights, and trust—not by hoping someone will move fast despite the system.

The goal isn't speed for its own sake. It's matching decision velocity to market velocity. When the world moves fast, slow decisions are expensive decisions—no matter how carefully they're made.

Actions for Readers: The Speed Transformation

The Speed Audit:

Track your decision velocity for one week. For every decision made (or delayed):

- How long from "we need to decide" to actual decision?
- How many people were involved?
- How many meetings did it take?
- Was this reversible or irreversible?
- Did speed match stakes?

After one week: What % of decisions were reversible but treated as irreversible? That's your speed opportunity.

Day 1-3: The Reversibility Test

For the next three decisions you face:

Before discussing: Ask yourself: "If this decision is wrong, can we reverse it easily?"

- **If YES (two-way door):** Set a 48-hour deadline for deciding. Move fast.
- **If NO (one-way door):** Take time. Gather input. Be thorough.

Practice treating two-way doors differently. Most decisions are more reversible than we think.

Week 1: Install Speed Infrastructure

Monday: Name DRIs for your top 5 recurring decision types

- Who decides about hiring? (HR leader)
- Who decides about budget allocation under $X? (Department leads)
- Who decides about process changes? (Process owners)
- Make it explicit. Post it publicly.

Tuesday: Eliminate one approval layer

- Find one decision type that currently requires your sign-off
- Can it be safely delegated? If yes, delegate it completely.
- Define boundaries, then step back.

Wednesday: Run the "silent meeting" test

- In your next decision meeting, stay silent for the first 20 minutes
- Let others debate, question, decide
- Only speak if the decision authority asks for your input
- Notice: Did your silence slow or speed the decision?

Thursday: Replace one meeting with a memo

- Pick your next "update" or "status" meeting
- Cancel it. Ask for a written memo instead.
- Read it. Ask questions asynchronously. Decide.
- Measure: Time saved vs. quality of decision.

Friday: The speed retrospective

- Which decisions moved faster this week?
- Which decisions took longer than they should have?
- What friction did you remove? What remains?

Month 1: Build Speed Habits

Implement the two-pizza rule for decision meetings:

- 8 people maximum in any decision meeting
- If more input needed, collect it before the meeting
- Make decisions with small groups, communicate broadly

Create the "decide by" norm:

- Every discussion starts with: "We'll decide this by [date/time]"
- If new information emerges, deadline can shift
- But there's always a decision deadline visible

Practice "disagree and commit" publicly:

- When you disagree with a decision, say so clearly during debate
- When the decision is made, commit fully to execution
- Model that disagreement ≠ disloyalty

Month 2-3: Transform Decision Culture

Measure and publish decision velocity:

- Average time from "need to decide" to "decided"
- % of decisions made in first meeting vs. requiring multiple meetings
- % of decisions reversed (if low, you're moving too slowly—not enough experimentation)

Celebrate fast good decisions:

- When someone makes a fast decision on a two-way door, recognize it

- When a decision gets reversed and we learn from it, celebrate the learning
- When teams decide without escalating, highlight their ownership

Address decision-avoidance:

- When people say "we need more data," ask: "What decision would that data change?"
- When people say "let's schedule another meeting," ask: "What will be different then?"
- When people say "we need consensus," ask: "Who's the DRI?"

The 90-Day Challenge:

Pick one area where decisions are painfully slow. Track current baseline (how long does X decision typically take?). Implement speed practices systematically. Measure after 90 days.

Target: 50% reduction in decision cycle time while maintaining (or improving) decision quality.

If you hit it, scale the practices. If you miss it, diagnose why—was it real vs. fake empowerment? Unclear DRIs? Cultural resistance? Learn and adjust.

A Final Reflection

That product launch taught me something fundamental: the cost of slow decisions is invisible until you calculate what you lose while deliberating.

Every day we delayed was a day competitors moved forward. Every meeting we scheduled to "review one more time" was a week customers went without the solution we'd built. Every consensus-seeking loop was an opportunity lost.

Ten years ago, I would have defended the deliberate process. "We're being thorough. We're managing risk. We're building alignment."

Now I understand: we were being afraid. Afraid of being wrong. Afraid of being blamed. Afraid of the discomfort that comes with deciding before we feel certain.

But certainty is an illusion. No amount of analysis guarantees success. The market doesn't wait for you to feel ready. Competitors don't pause while you build consensus.

The organizations that win aren't the ones with perfect decisions. They're the ones with fast decisions, fast learning, and fast adaptation. They treat speed as strategy, not just efficiency.

The next time you're in a meeting where everyone agrees we need "just one more week to think about it," ask yourself: What's the cost of that week? What are we learning during deliberation that we couldn't learn faster through action?

Sometimes the answer is "this needs more time." But often, more often than we admit, the answer is that we're stalling because deciding feels uncomfortable.

Speed isn't recklessness. It's matching decision velocity to actual reversibility. It's having the courage to move when movement matters more than certainty.

Your next competitive advantage might not come from better strategy. It might come from deciding and executing before your competitors finish their third review meeting.

Chapter 10
The Audacity Operating System

"I'M ASKING FOR 50 CRORE TO INVEST IN MY LEMONADE STAND."

The Strategy That Felt Small

The product strategy review had been going for ninety minutes. The recommendation: incremental improvements to our existing offering. Add features customers requested. Improve performance. Refine the interface.

It made sense. Low risk. Predictable returns. No one could criticize the logic.

But it also felt... small. We were optimizing the present at the expense of the future.

I stopped the presentation. "This is a good plan for maintaining what we have. But what if we're thinking too small? What if the real opportunity isn't improving our current product, it's reimagining what the product could be?"

The room went quiet. People shifted uncomfortably. The VP of Product looked confused: "We spent three months developing this strategy. We validated it with customers. The data supports it."

"I'm not questioning the data," I said. "I'm questioning our ambition. What would we do if we were willing to be bold?"

The conversation that followed was uncomfortable. People pushed back. The proposed incremental strategy was safe, achievable, and defensible. Going bolder meant risk: the risk of failure, wasted resources, and looking foolish if it didn't work.

But over the next two hours, something shifted. We started asking different questions. Not "What can we safely improve?" but "What could we transform?" Not "What do customers say they want?" but "What problem could we solve that they haven't imagined?"

By the end, we'd sketched a fundamentally different approach, one that would require rebuilding core parts of the product, challenging our business model, and betting on an unproven market hypothesis.

It was audacious. It was risky. And six months later, it became our fastest-growing product line and opened markets we'd never accessed before.

Chapter 10
The Audacity Operating System

That day taught me something crucial: the biggest risk isn't bold bets that might fail. It's safe bets that guarantee you'll never transform.

What Audacity Actually Means

Audacity isn't recklessness. It's not ignoring data, gambling blindly, or moving fast without thinking.

Audacity is calculated ambition. It's making bold bets based on conviction, not certainty. It's challenging assumptions everyone accepts while respecting facts everyone knows. It's being willing to be spectacularly wrong in pursuit of being transformatively right.

The distinction matters because most organizations confuse prudence with paralysis. They avoid bold moves not because the risks are unmanageable, but because boldness feels uncomfortable.

I've watched companies die slowly, not from dramatic failures, but from incremental decline disguised as stability. They optimized what they had while the market moved past them. They made safe choices quarter after quarter until those choices became obsolete.

The organizations that thrive aren't the ones that avoid risk. They're the ones that take calculated risks before they're forced to take desperate ones.

The Foundation: Trust and Safety

Audacity requires trust as a foundation—the operating system. You can't encourage bold moves while punishing failure. Without trust, people default to safe choices. With it, they lean into ambitious bets.

Psychological safety is what makes audacity possible at scale. People take bold risks when they trust that intelligent failures won't be punished. Without safety, audacity becomes career suicide.

I learned this watching a team struggle after we'd announced we wanted "more bold thinking." Leaders said it. But when someone proposed an audacious idea that didn't work, they got quietly sidelined from important projects. The message was clear: we say we want boldness, but we punish it when it fails.

Audacity died immediately. People went back to safe proposals dressed up with ambitious language. We got performance, not conviction.

Real audacity requires making failure safe—not comfortable, but safe. You can fail intelligently without derailing your career. You can take big swings knowing that even if you miss, you're valued for trying.

What Audacity Is Not

Before going further, let me clarify what audacity isn't—because the distinction between calculated audacity and destructive behavior matters:

Not recklessness. Audacity is calculated risk based on conviction. Recklessness is risk without thinking. Audacity asks "What could go right and how do we maximize that possibility?" Recklessness ignores "What could go wrong?"

Not ignoring reality. Audacity challenges assumptions, but respects facts. It asks "What if we're wrong about the constraints?" not "Let's ignore constraints." It's grounded in reality even while reaching for possibility.

Not stubbornness. Audacity pivots when evidence contradicts the bet. Stubbornness doubles down regardless of results. Audacity says "I'll commit fully to this bold path, and change course if I'm wrong." Stubbornness says "I'm right no matter what the data shows."

Enabling Audacity: Reversibility

The two-door framework enables audacity: when decisions are reversible, bold experiments become safe. The cost of being wrong is low, so the barrier to trying is low.

This transformed how we approached product development. Instead of debating for months whether a bold feature would work, we'd prototype it in two weeks, test it with customers, and learn. If it worked, we'd double down. If it didn't, we'd kill it fast.

The cost of trying was low. The cost of not trying—of letting competitors experiment while we debated—was high.

SpaceX embodies this principle. Elon Musk's approach to rocket development wasn't "design the perfect rocket through extensive analysis." It was "build, test, explode, learn, iterate." Rockets blew up spectacularly. Each explosion taught lessons that no amount of theoretical modeling could provide.

The audacity wasn't in accepting explosions. It was in designing for rapid iteration, making each failure cheap enough and informative enough to justify the bold experimentation.

The Build vs. Buy Decision

One moment crystallized this principle for me. We needed a specialized technology platform. The safe choice: buy from an established vendor. Proven solution, predictable costs, minimal risk.

The audacious choice: build it ourselves. Higher risk, longer timeline, significant resource investment. But also: exactly what we needed, competitive advantage, and learning that would benefit other initiatives.

The debate was intense. Finance preferred buying (lower upfront cost, faster deployment). Engineering wanted to build (more control, better long-term fit). The decision kept getting postponed because neither side could prove their approach was "right."

Finally, I reframed the question: "Is this reversible?"

The answer: mostly yes. If we built and it failed, we could buy later. We'd lose time and money, but we wouldn't be locked into an irreversible path.

That changed everything. Instead of requiring certainty that building would work, we only needed conviction it was worth trying. We had that.

We built. It took longer than projected. It cost more than budgeted. And it became a core competitive advantage that differentiated us for years.

The audacity wasn't blind optimism. It was calculated risk-taking based on understanding reversibility.

Building the Audacity Muscle

Audacity isn't a switch you flip. It's a muscle you build through progressive practice. Here's how we developed it organizationally:

Stage 1: Small bets build confidence. We started with low-stakes experiments where failure was cheap. Test a new approach to customer onboarding. Try a different pricing model for one segment. Experiment with an unconventional marketing message.

Each small success built confidence. Each small failure that didn't destroy us taught that risk was manageable.

Stage 2: Visible experiments normalize boldness. Once small bets worked, we made experiments more visible. We'd pilot bold approaches, share results broadly (including failures), and celebrate the learning process.

This normalized risk-taking. People saw that trying bold things—even when they didn't work—was valued, not punished.

Stage 3: Big bets leverage confidence. With small-bet muscles built, we started making larger commitments. Enter a new market. Rebuild a core platform. Restructure how we worked with clients.

These weren't reckless. They were informed by learning from smaller experiments and enabled by cultural confidence that intelligent failure was acceptable.

Stage 4: Embed in systems. Finally, we made audacity structural, not situational. Strategic planning required including transformative bets alongside incremental improvements. Resource allocation included an "audacity budget" for bold experiments. Performance reviews assessed risk-taking, not just safe execution.

Stage 5: Make it sustainable. The goal wasn't permanent adrenaline. It was building organizational capability for calculated boldness—knowing when to be audacious and when to be prudent, but defaulting to boldness when stakes and reversibility align.

When Audacity Goes Right

Airbnb's founding bet was audacious to the point of seeming absurd. Convince strangers to stay in other strangers' homes. Challenge century-old hospitality models. Build trust at scale in contexts designed for suspicion.

Investors said it would never work. Regulatory frameworks opposed it. Common wisdom declared it dangerous.

But the founders had conviction based on their own experience. They'd rented out air mattresses in their apartment and discovered people were willing to try. They had a reversible hypothesis: if trust couldn't be built, they'd learn fast and pivot.

They leaned into the audacity. They didn't water down the vision to make it palatable. They committed fully to the bold bet.

It worked not because they were lucky, but because they combined conviction with rapid learning. They failed constantly—bad listings, trust violations, regulatory battles—but each failure taught them how to make the model work.

That's audacity: bold bets informed by conviction, enabled by reversibility, and refined through learning.

The Audacity Killers

Beyond the consensus requirements, analysis paralysis, and hero culture that kill bold thinking, three patterns specifically destroy audacity:

1. Punishing intelligent failure. When mistakes from bold bets carry career consequences, people choose safety. A VP who backs a transformative initiative that fails gets quietly moved aside. A team that tries an ambitious approach that doesn't work loses future opportunities.

The message is clear: audacity is career suicide. People learn to propose safe ideas with bold language, not actual bold ideas.

Fix: Separate intelligent failure from negligence. Bold bets that don't work are learning opportunities. Repeatedly ignoring evidence or taking reckless risks has consequences. Make the distinction explicit and enforce it consistently.

2. Short-term metrics dominance. When quarterly results are the only measure, transformative bets that take years can't get funded. The system rewards incrementalism because it shows up in this quarter's numbers. Audacity gets deprioritized because benefits are distant.

Fix: Create dual metrics. Track quarterly performance AND long-term transformative bets. Allocate resources explicitly for both. Make it legitimate to invest in bold initiatives with multi-year payoffs.

3. No permission to think big. When "be realistic" is code for "don't challenge assumptions," audacity dies. People self-censor before ideas are even voiced. Meetings reward incrementalism and punish imagination.

Fix: Create explicit space for audacious thinking. Start planning sessions with "What would we do if we had permission to be bold?" before constraining with reality. Let ideas breathe before judging feasibility.

The Audacity Spectrum

Risk vs. Ambition

Paralysis	Safe Incrementalism	Calculated Audacity	Recklessness	Chaos
All ideas feel too risky	Predictable improvements	Sweet spot	Bold without thinking	No strategy, just action
Analysis without action	Low risk, low transformation	Reversible where possible	Ignore evidence	Change for change's sake
Decline disguised as stability	Maintain but never leap	Learn fast, pivot or scale	Gamble, don't calculate	Burn resources randomly

Risk → Ambition

Building Permission

One of the most powerful levers for enabling audacity: explicit permission to think big.

I started ending strategic planning sessions with a different question. Not "What should we do?" but "What would we do if we knew we couldn't fail?"

The first few times, people looked confused. That question felt like fantasy, not strategy.

But gradually, something shifted. People started voicing ideas they'd been self-censoring. Bold possibilities they'd dismissed as "unrealistic" before even sharing them.

Most of those ideas were, in fact, unrealistic. But buried among them were a few genuinely transformative possibilities—opportunities we'd never have considered if we'd started with constraints.

Once ideas were on the table, we could work backward: "This feels too ambitious. What would need to be true to make it feasible? Are any of those things actually possible?"

Sometimes the answer was no. But occasionally, we'd discover that what felt impossible was just unfamiliar. The constraints we assumed were immovable turned out to be negotiable.

That shift—from "be realistic" to "what if we could be bold?"—unlocked thinking that incremental planning never would.

The Transformation Timeline

Building an audacity culture doesn't happen overnight. Here's what it actually looked like:

Quarter 1: Small visible experiments. Pilots that carried some risk but were reversible. Some worked, some didn't. We shared results openly—including failures.

Quarter 2: Bolder initiatives. Projects that required real resources and commitment. Not all succeeded, but we celebrated the learning from failures.

Quarter 3: First major transformative bet. Significant resources, meaningful risk. Leadership committed publicly. Success wasn't guaranteed, but we were all-in.

Quarter 4: Results starting to show. Some bets paid off. Some didn't. But the organization had learned that bold thinking was valued and intelligent failure was safe.

Year 2: Audacity became normal. Bold proposals weren't unusual—they were expected in strategic planning. The muscle had been built.

The Moment It Worked

Three years into building audacity culture, a junior product manager proposed something that would have been killed immediately in our old culture.

She wanted to completely reimagine how customers interacted with our core platform. Not incremental improvement—fundamental redesign. It required significant engineering resources, risked disrupting current users, and challenged assumptions about how our product worked.

In our old culture, this would have been dismissed as unrealistic, too risky, or "not understanding how things work here."

Instead, the conversation was different: "Walk us through your thinking. What makes you believe this could work? What would we need to learn to test it? How could we make it reversible?"

She'd done her homework. She had conviction based on customer research. She'd identified ways to test assumptions cheaply. She'd thought through reversibility.

Chapter 10
The Audacity Operating System

We funded a two-month proof of concept. It worked well enough to justify a bigger bet. Six months later, it became one of our most successful feature launches.

What struck me wasn't just that the feature succeeded. It was that a junior person felt empowered to propose something audacious, and the organization had the muscle to evaluate it on merits rather than dismissing it as too bold.

That's when I knew the culture had shifted. Audacity wasn't a special initiative anymore. It was how we operated.

Actions for Readers: Building Your Audacity Practice

The Audacity Assessment:

Rate your last 5 major decisions on a scale: 1 = Completely safe, no risk 5 = Moderately bold, some risk 10 = Audaciously ambitious, significant risk

Average score:

- Below 3: You're playing too safe
- 3-5: You're balancing, but may be missing transformative opportunities
- 5-7: Healthy risk appetite
- Above 7: Verify it's calculated audacity, not recklessness

The Small Bets Ladder (Weeks 1-4):

Build audacity muscle with progressively bolder experiments:

Week 1 - The Micro-Bet: Make one decision that feels 20% bolder than normal. Examples:

- Propose an idea you've been holding back

- Test an approach others think won't work
- Challenge an assumption everyone accepts Make it reversible. Track what happens.

Week 2 - The Visible Experiment: Try something bold enough that others notice. Examples:

- Pitch a project outside your normal scope
- Advocate for an unpopular position in a meeting
- Propose eliminating something everyone assumes is necessary. Make it public. Own the outcome.

Week 3 - The Team Bet: Involve your team in a bold initiative. Examples:

- Give someone a stretch assignment beyond their experience
- Greenlight an experiment you're skeptical about
- Challenge your team to solve a problem you think is impossible Support them. Celebrate learning regardless of results.

Week 4 - The Intelligent Failure: Try something with real possibility of visible failure. Examples:

- Present a half-formed idea to leadership
- Launch an experiment without perfect data
- Make a bet where failure would be obvious Own it. Share what you learned publicly.

Month 2: The Bold Bet

Identify one audacious initiative for your area. Characteristics:

- Would transform outcomes if it worked (not incremental improvement)
- Has real risk of failure

- Challenges current assumptions
- Requires resources or authority you'll need to advocate for

Build the case:

- What's the bold vision? (Not "improve X by 20%" but "fundamentally change X")
- Why now? (What's the opportunity cost of not trying?)
- What's the reversibility? (How do you know if it's failing and can you course-correct?)
- What do you need? (Resources, authority, air cover)

Pitch it. Expect resistance. That's how you know it's actually bold.

Month 3: Build the Audacity Culture

Make audacity visible:

- Start team meetings with: "What's one bold idea we should consider?"
- End retrospectives with: "What bold bet could we make next?"
- Recognize people who propose ambitious ideas, not just those who execute safe plans

Celebrate intelligent failures publicly:

- When a bold bet fails, hold a "learning session" not a post-mortem
- Extract lessons, share them broadly, thank the risk-taker
- Make it clear: career consequences come from not trying bold things, not from trying and learning

Create the "Audacity Budget":

- Allocate 10-15% of resources explicitly for bold experiments
- Expect half to fail

- Measure learning, not just success
- Protect this budget from being raided for "safe" uses

Quarter 2-4: Embed in Operations

Integrate into planning:

- Every strategic plan must include at least one "transformative bet" alongside incremental improvements
- Quarterly reviews must assess: Are we being bold enough?
- Incentives must reward intelligent risk-taking, not just safe execution

Develop risk literacy:

- Teach teams the two-door framework*
- Practice distinguishing calculated audacity from recklessness
- Build muscle around "What would we try if failure wasn't shameful?"

Measure what matters:

- Track: % of initiatives that are transformative vs. incremental
- Track: Ratio of bold bets to safe plays
- Track: Number of intelligent failures we learned from
- Track: Ideas proposed by team (volume and boldness)

If all metrics trend safe, you're not building audacity—you're performing it.

A Closing Reflection

That product strategy meeting taught me something I wish I'd learned earlier: the biggest risk in leadership isn't bold bets that might fail. It's safe bets that guarantee mediocrity.

Chapter 10
The Audacity Operating System

Organizations don't die from spectacular failures. They die from incremental decline—from playing it safe quarter after quarter until safe choices become obsolete.

Ten years ago, I would have approved that incremental product strategy. It was defensible. It was data-driven. Nobody could criticize the logic.

Now I understand: defensible isn't the goal. Transformation is. And transformation requires audacity—calculated, informed, reversible where possible—but audacity nonetheless.

> *The question isn't "What's the safest thing we can do?" It is "What's the boldest thing we can do responsibly?"*

The next time you're in a strategy session where every proposal feels safe, ask yourself: Are we being prudent, or are we being afraid? Are we managing risk, or are we avoiding opportunity?

Because in fast-moving markets, the riskiest strategy is having no audacious bets at all.

Your competitors are making bold moves. Your market is shifting rapidly. Your customers' needs are evolving faster than incremental improvements can address.

The organizations that win won't be the ones that played it safest. They'll be the ones that calculated intelligently, bet boldly, learned quickly, and pivoted or scaled based on results.

That's not recklessness. That's leadership.

And it requires audacity.

Part 3
Sustaining the Future : Leadership Beyond Presence

Chapter 11
AI as Co-Leader

"YES — THAT'S OUR HUMAN IN THE LOOP."

The Customer Service Crisis

The customer service organization was drowning. Call volumes had grown 40% in eighteen months. Customer satisfaction was declining. Wait times were increasing. The team was burned out.

The obvious solution: hire more people. We'd need 50+ customer service representatives at a cost of several million dollars annually.

But there was another option: AI-powered customer service handling routine inquiries, freeing human agents for complex issues requiring judgment and empathy.

The debate was heated. Some leaders worried AI would degrade customer experience. Others feared the team would resist technology that "replaced" them. Still others questioned whether AI could actually handle our specific customer needs.

We ran a three-month pilot. AI handled tier-one inquiries, password resets, account questions, basic troubleshooting. Human agents handled escalations, complex problems, and situations requiring empathy.

The results surprised even the optimists:

- 60% of inquiries resolved by AI without human involvement
- Average resolution time dropped from 18 minutes to 4 minutes
- Customer satisfaction improved (faster resolution for simple issues)
- Agent satisfaction improved (less repetitive work, more meaningful interactions)
- Cost per inquiry dropped 40%

But the most striking finding: the human agents became more effective, not less relevant. Freed from routine inquiries, they handled complex problems that genuinely needed human judgment. Their job became more interesting, more valued, and more impactful.

That pilot taught me something fundamental: AI isn't a threat to leadership, it's a capability multiplier. The question isn't whether to use AI, but how to partner with it effectively.

Chapter 11
AI as Co-Leader

From Tool to Colleague

Most leaders treat AI as a tool, something you use occasionally for specific tasks, like using a calculator or a spreadsheet.

That's a fundamental misunderstanding.

AI isn't a tool. It's a colleague. Not in the sense of having consciousness or emotions, but in the sense of having capabilities you can delegate to, work alongside, and collaborate with to achieve outcomes.

The shift in mindset matters. When you treat AI as a tool, you think: "What task can I automate?" When you treat AI as a colleague, you think: "What outcomes can I delegate?"

I learned this through experience. Initially, I used AI for discrete tasks: "Summarize these meeting notes." "Draft this email." "Analyze this data set."

Useful, but limited. I was still doing all the thinking, AI was just executing pieces.

The transformation came when I started delegating outcomes, not tasks. Instead of "Summarize these customer reviews," I'd say: "Analyze customer feedback from the last quarter and identify the top three themes causing dissatisfaction, with supporting evidence and preliminary recommendations."

The difference: AI wasn't just executing, it was thinking, analyzing, synthesizing. I was delegating judgment-requiring work while maintaining oversight and accountability.

The Delegation Framework for AI

Delegating to AI requires the same fundamentals as delegating to any capable colleague: clear outcomes, defined boundaries, accountability for results. You don't micromanage how, you specify what and why, then let them figure out the approach.

Here's what effective delegation to AI looks like:

1. Define the outcome, not the process. Bad: "Read these reports and extract key points." Better: "Analyze these quarterly reports and identify strategic risks we're not adequately addressing, with evidence from each report."

The first treats AI as a task-executor. The second treats it as an analytical partner.

2. Set clear boundaries. What can AI decide autonomously? What requires human approval? What data can it access?

For our customer service AI, boundaries were explicit: Handle tier-one inquiries independently. Escalate anything involving account security, legal concerns, or significant customer dissatisfaction. Never make promises about future product features or pricing.

3. Establish feedback loops. How do you verify AI is performing well? How does AI improve based on your input?

We spot-checked 5% of AI-resolved customer inquiries weekly. When AI made mistakes, we fed corrections back into the system. Over time, performance improved as AI learned from our judgment.

4. Maintain accountability. You're accountable for AI's outputs, just as you're accountable for work your team produces. AI doesn't diminish your responsibility, it extends your capability.

Chapter 11
AI as Co-Leader

Building Trust in AI Systems

Trust in AI develops the same way trust in people does: verify but don't micromanage, create feedback loops, establish clear accountability. The difference: you're building trust in a system, not a person.

Early in our AI journey, I made the mistake of either over-trusting or under-trusting. I'd either accept AI outputs without verification (dangerous) or second-guess everything (defeating the purpose).

The breakthrough came from treating AI like a talented but junior colleague: trust their work in areas where they've proven capable, verify their work in higher-stakes situations, and recognize the boundaries of their competence.

Over time, I learned AI's strengths and limitations in our specific context. AI was exceptional at pattern recognition across large data sets, tireless at repetitive analysis, and fast at generating alternatives. But AI struggled with novel situations, context-dependent judgment, and situations requiring empathy or ethical reasoning.

Understanding those boundaries let me delegate appropriately: fully trust AI for tasks in its competence zone, verify carefully when approaching boundaries, never delegate tasks beyond its capability.

What AI Is Exceptional At

Through experimentation, I've identified where AI genuinely excels:

Pattern recognition at scale. AI can identify trends, anomalies, and correlations across data volumes humans can't process. Customer behavior patterns, operational inefficiencies, market signals buried in noise, AI sees patterns we'd miss.

Tireless analysis. AI doesn't get fatigued, distracted, or bored. It can analyze hundreds of resumes, thousands of customer reviews, or millions of data points with consistent quality.

Speed. What takes humans days or weeks, AI completes in minutes. Competitive analysis, market research synthesis, scenario modeling—AI compresses timelines dramatically.

Option generation. AI can generate alternatives you haven't considered. "Here are twelve approaches to this problem" often includes perspectives that wouldn't have occurred to you.

Knowledge synthesis. AI can pull together information from disparate sources, research papers, industry reports, internal documents, and synthesize insights across domains.

What AI Struggles With

Equally important: understanding AI's limitations.

Novel situations. AI learns from patterns in existing data. When facing genuinely new situations without precedent, AI struggles. Human judgment based on principles and analogies often outperforms AI extrapolation.

Context-dependent judgment. AI lacks lived experience. It can't "read the room," understand organizational politics, or navigate complex interpersonal dynamics.

Ethical reasoning. AI can identify ethical dilemmas but can't resolve them. Questions of values, fairness, and competing priorities require human judgment.

Empathy and emotional intelligence. AI can simulate empathy but doesn't feel it. Customer situations requiring genuine care and team dynamics needing emotional support require humans.

Strategic intuition. The "gut feel" based on years of experience, the ability to sense when something's off despite data suggesting otherwise, this remains deeply human.

The Partnership Model

The goal isn't AI replacing humans or humans constraining AI. It's strategic partnership where each contributes their strengths.

Here's how I've learned to structure the partnership:

AI for breadth, humans for depth. AI analyzes all customer feedback, identifies top themes. Humans dive deep into the most important themes, understanding nuance and context AI misses.

AI for speed, humans for judgment. AI screens all job applicants in hours, flagging top candidates based on objective criteria. Humans interview finalists, assessing cultural fit and potential that resumes don't capture.

AI for options, humans for choice. AI generates strategic alternatives with pros/cons analysis. Humans choose based on values, risk appetite, and contextual factors AI can't fully evaluate.

AI for monitoring, humans for response. AI watches for operational anomalies, customer satisfaction drops, or market shifts. Humans investigate and respond based on strategic priorities.

The Five Stages of AI Integration

Organizations typically evolve through stages in their AI capability:

Stage 1: Automation. Replace repetitive, rules-based tasks. Data entry, basic categorization, simple responses. Low-hanging fruit with clear ROI.

Stage 2: Augmentation. Enhance human capability with AI analysis. Humans make decisions, but with AI-powered insights they couldn't generate manually. Most organizations operate here.

Stage 3: Analysis. AI identifies patterns and insights humans would miss. Not just faster analysis, but genuinely better pattern recognition across complexity. Requires high-quality data and clear analytical goals.

Stage 4: Recommendation. AI doesn't just analyze, it recommends actions. Humans retain decision authority but AI suggests what to do, not just what's happening. Requires strong trust and validation systems.

Stage 5: Delegation. AI owns specific outcomes with defined boundaries and human oversight. Not AI deciding everything, but AI having genuine autonomy within its domain. Requires mature processes and organizational comfort with AI partnership.

Most organizations should aim for Stage 3-4. Stage 5 is appropriate for specific use cases but shouldn't be default.

When AI Partnerships Fail

I've watched AI initiatives fail spectacularly. The patterns are instructive.

Over-reliance without verification. A hiring manager used AI resume screening but didn't validate the criteria AI was optimizing for. Six months later, we discovered AI had systematically screened out candidates from non-traditional backgrounds because our historical hiring data was biased. We weren't getting diverse candidates because AI had learned to replicate our past biases.

Chapter 11
AI as Co-Leader

Under-trust that defeats the purpose. A team implemented AI for contract review but required human lawyers to review every AI output in detail. The "efficiency gain" disappeared because we were doing work twice. Either trust AI for appropriate tasks or don't use it—half-measures waste resources.

Unclear accountability. When AI recommended a strategic move that failed, the leadership team debated: Was this the DRI's fault for following AI's recommendation? Or AI's fault for bad analysis? The ambiguity paralyzed future AI use.

The lesson: accountability must be clear. Leaders are accountable for AI outputs just as they're accountable for team outputs. AI is a capability you deploy, not an entity that bears responsibility.

"The goal isn't using AI everywhere. It's using AI optimally—delegating where it excels, partnering where judgment matters."

Building AI Literacy

The biggest barrier to effective AI use isn't technology, it's organizational capability.

Leaders need AI literacy: understanding what AI can and can't do, when to use it, how to evaluate outputs, and where human judgment remains essential.

We built AI literacy through practice, not training. Instead of sending people to AI courses, we created learning-by-doing opportunities:

Monthly "AI experiments" where teams tried AI for specific use cases and shared results (including failures). This normalized experimentation and built practical knowledge.

AI Champions in each department who became go-to resources for "Could AI help with this?" questions. Not AI experts, just people comfortable experimenting.

Failure retrospectives when AI didn't work, focusing on what we learned rather than who to blame. This made it safe to try bold AI applications.

Over time, AI capability built organically. People learned through use, not through abstract instruction.

The Ethical Questions

AI raises ethical questions that don't have easy answers.

Bias and fairness. AI learns from data, and data reflects historical biases. If your hiring data is biased, AI will learn those biases. The solution isn't avoiding AI, it's actively identifying and correcting biases in both data and AI outputs.

Transparency. When AI makes recommendations, can you understand why? "Black box" AI that can't explain its reasoning is dangerous for high-stakes decisions. Explainability matters.

Accountability. When AI-assisted decisions go wrong, who's responsible? The answer must be clear: the human leader who deployed AI and validated (or failed to validate) its outputs.

Job displacement. AI will eliminate some jobs and transform others. Pretending otherwise is dishonest. The responsible approach: help people develop AI-adjacent skills, create new roles that leverage human+AI capabilities, and be honest about changes coming.

Data privacy. What data can AI access? How is it stored? Who can see AI's analysis? These aren't technical questions, they're values questions requiring human judgment.

I don't have perfect answers. But I've learned that ignoring ethical questions doesn't make them go away, it just ensures you'll address them reactively after problems emerge rather than proactively before deployment.

The Human+AI Future

The question isn't "Will AI replace leaders?" It's "What does leadership look like when AI is your analytical co-leader?"

I've come to see AI as fundamentally expanding leadership capacity. With AI handling analysis, pattern recognition, and option generation, leaders can focus on what remains uniquely human: judgment in ambiguity, empathy in complexity, values in trade-offs, and vision beyond data.

The leaders who thrive won't be the ones who resist AI or the ones who blindly trust it. They'll be the ones who learn to partner effectively, delegating where AI excels, applying human judgment where it matters, and combining both to achieve outcomes neither could reach alone.

Five years ago, I spent hours analyzing data to prepare for strategic decisions. Now AI does that analysis in minutes, and I spend hours on what AI can't do: understanding stakeholder dynamics, evaluating ethical implications, building organizational support, and making judgment calls where values conflict.

My leadership capacity hasn't diminished—it's been redirected toward higher-value activities.

> *That's the future: not AI replacing leaders, but AI freeing leaders to focus on what actually requires human leadership.*

A Closing Story

Last quarter, we faced a complex market entry decision. Multiple variables, incomplete data, significant resource commitment required.

In the past, this would have consumed weeks of analysis—gathering data, building models, debating scenarios. We'd have made the decision based on inevitably imperfect analysis because perfection was impossible given time constraints.

Instead, I delegated the analytical work to AI: "Analyze market entry options across these three regions. For each, assess market size, competitive intensity, regulatory barriers, customer acquisition costs, and potential ROI under optimistic, realistic, and pessimistic scenarios. Identify key assumptions underlying each scenario and flag where data quality is weakest."

After a few iterations, AI delivered a comprehensive analysis in a matter of hours, work that would have taken our team three weeks and still been less thorough.

But AI didn't make the decision. It couldn't weigh our risk appetite, strategic priorities, organizational capability to execute in different regions, or alignment with long-term vision.

That's where human leadership came in. Armed with AI's analysis, our leadership team spent two days debating trade-offs, evaluating against strategic priorities, stress-testing assumptions, and ultimately making the call.

We made a better decision faster. Not because AI replaced our judgment, but because it extended our analytical capability, freeing us to focus on judgment, strategy, and values.

That's the partnership working as it should.

Actions for Readers: Your AI Integration Journey

The AI Readiness Assessment:

Evaluate your current state across four dimensions:

1. Use Cases (0-10 scale):

- Do you have clear problems AI could solve? (Not "use AI" but "solve X problem")
- Score: 0 = No identified use cases → 10 = Multiple prioritized opportunities

2. Data Infrastructure (0-10 scale):

- Do you have accessible, clean data AI can learn from?
- Score: 0 = Data chaos → 10 = Well-structured, accessible data

3. Team Capability (0-10 scale):

- Does your team understand AI capabilities and limitations?

- Score: 0 = No AI literacy → 10 = Strong AI fluency

4. Cultural Readiness (0-10 scale):

- Is your organization open to AI-human collaboration?
- Score: 0 = AI-hostile culture → 10 = Experimentation-friendly

Total score interpretation:

- 0-15: Build foundation before deploying AI
- 16-25: Ready for targeted pilots
- 26-35: Ready for broader integration
- 36-40: Ready for advanced AI partnership

Phase 1: The First AI Experiment (Weeks 1-4)

Don't start with "AI strategy." Start with one small experiment.

Week 1 - Identify the pilot: Pick ONE repetitive, data-intensive task that:

- Takes significant human time
- Follows clear patterns
- Has measurable outcomes
- Won't break things if AI makes mistakes

Examples:

- Summarizing customer feedback themes
- First-pass resume screening
- Basic data analysis and visualization
- Meeting notes and action item extraction

Week 2 - Choose and deploy a tool:

- Don't build custom AI (yet)

- Use existing tools: ChatGPT, Claude, Gemini, or specialized platforms
- Give one person ownership of the pilot
- Set a 2-week trial period

Week 3-4 - Measure and learn:

- Time saved vs. quality maintained
- What worked? What didn't?
- Where did AI need human override?
- What surprised you (positively and negatively)?

Critical: Share results publicly, including failures

Phase 2: Expanding AI Use (Month 2-3)

Based on pilot learnings, expand thoughtfully.

Identify 3-5 more use cases across different functions:

- Customer-facing (service, sales, marketing)
- Internal operations (HR, finance, admin)
- Strategic work (analysis, planning, research)

For each use case, define:

- What outcome you're optimizing for (not "use AI" but "reduce X time by Y%")
- What AI will do vs. what humans will do
- How you'll measure success
- What governance/oversight is needed

Build AI literacy systematically:

- Monthly "AI Show and Tell" - teams demo what they're trying

- Create "AI Champions" who help others experiment
- Share failures as learning opportunities, not embarrassments

Phase 3: Delegation Framework (Month 3-4)

Move from AI as tool to AI as delegated capability.

For each AI application, define:

1. Clear outcome: What result do you need? (Not "analyze data" but "identify top 3 customer pain points from feedback")

2. Boundaries: What constraints must AI respect?

- Data it can/can't access
- Decisions it can make vs. must escalate
- Quality thresholds that trigger human review

3. Accountability: How do you verify AI is performing?

- Spot-check process (what % of AI outputs do humans review?)
- Quality metrics (accuracy, relevance, usefulness)
- Feedback loops (how does AI improve based on human corrections?)

Create "AI task sheets" similar to job descriptions:

- Task: [What AI is responsible for]
- Authority: [What AI can decide autonomously]
- Escalation: [When AI must involve humans]
- Success metrics: [How performance is measured]

Phase 4: Cultural Integration (Month 4-6)

Make AI partnership normal, not special.

Chapter 11
AI as Co-Leader

Embed in workflows:

- Strategy sessions: "What analysis should we ask AI to run?"
- Problem-solving: "Could AI help us see patterns we're missing?"
- Decision reviews: "Did we use AI to stress-test our assumptions?"

Address resistance directly:

- Acknowledge fears about AI replacing jobs
- Show evidence of augmentation (AI + human > either alone)
- Recognize people who effectively partner with AI
- Make it clear: AI literacy is a career advantage, not threat

Establish governance:

- When does AI output need human approval?
- How do we handle AI mistakes or bias?
- What data can AI access?
- How do we ensure ethical AI use?

The Advanced Moves (Quarter 3-4):

Once AI partnership is established.

Strategic AI applications:

- Market analysis and opportunity identification
- Scenario planning and stress-testing strategies
- Competitive intelligence synthesis
- Customer insight mining at scale

AI in decision-making:

- Use AI to find blind spots in your reasoning
- Generate alternative perspectives you haven't considered

- Stress-test assumptions with data you'd miss manually
- Identify risks or opportunities buried in data

Build custom AI capabilities (only after mastering existing tools):

- Evaluate: Do existing tools meet 80% of needs?
- If yes, stick with them
- If no, consider custom solutions with clear ROI

Continuous Learning Loop:

Monthly AI review:

- What's working? Scale it.
- What's not working? Kill or pivot it.
- What new capabilities emerged? Experiment.
- What risks appeared? Address them.

Quarterly capability assessment:

- Are we using AI as effectively as we could?
- Where are we still doing manually what AI could handle?
- Where are we over-relying on AI and under-using human judgment?
- What's the next frontier for AI in our context?

A Final Reflection

That customer service transformation taught me something I initially resisted: AI isn't a threat to human capability, it's a multiplier of it.

The customer service agents weren't diminished when AI handled routine inquiries. They were elevated. Their work became more interesting, more valuable, more human. They solved problems that genuinely needed empathy, judgment, and creativity.

Ten years ago, I would have seen AI as automating people out of jobs. Now I understand: AI automates tasks that constrain people from doing their best work.

The future of leadership isn't "humans or AI." It's humans and AI—each contributing what they do best, in partnership that achieves what neither could alone.

The leaders who resist AI will find themselves outpaced by leaders who partner with it. The leaders who blindly trust AI will make catastrophic mistakes. The leaders who thrive will be the ones who learn the dance: delegate analysis to AI, apply judgment to choices, combine both for better decisions faster.

That's not replacing leadership. That's evolving it.

Your next competitive advantage might not come from working harder or hiring more people. It might come from learning to partner effectively with the most powerful analytical capability ever created.

The question isn't whether to use AI. It's whether you'll learn to use it well before your competitors do.

Chapter 12
From Silos to Pods

"Please rise and pledge allegiance to your department."

The Meeting I'll Never Forget

I knew we were in trouble when someone joked, "Maybe we need a committee to track our committees."

It was month six of what should have been a straightforward initiative—harmonizing financial reporting across regions. One version of truth. One reporting framework. Simple.

Except nothing about it felt simple anymore.

By the time I joined as an advisor, the project had earned a reputation inside the company. Not for breakthrough thinking or elegant solutions—but for the sheer bureaucratic stamina required to survive it.

Every decision needed seventeen sign-offs.

I remember the project manager showing me the approval workflow on a whiteboard during our first meeting. It looked less like governance and more like the circuit diagram of a malfunctioning machine, arrows looping everywhere, bottlenecks highlighted in red, waiting zones marked with acronyms I didn't recognize.

"If one person is on leave," he said with a tired smile, "the project pauses. If two people are on leave, it goes into hibernation."

The humor barely covered the exhaustion in his eyes.

In theory, the structure had been designed for accountability. In reality, it was engineered for delay. The organization had built a fortress against risk—and accidentally locked itself inside. Too many experts. Too many checkpoints. Too many invisible walls separating the exact functions that were supposed to collaborate.

It took four months just to approve the data taxonomy. By then, market conditions had shifted, priorities had changed, and everyone quietly pretended not to notice that we'd spent sixteen weeks debating field names while competitors were already shipping.

Chapter 12
From Silos to Pods

During one particularly tense steering committee meeting, I asked the CFO why the project had become so complex. Her answer stopped me:

"We built this structure to protect us from risk. Now it's the biggest risk we have."

That sentence captured the paradox I've seen in dozens of organizations since. The very systems we create to ensure control eventually start controlling us. We don't set out to build bureaucracy; we set out to build safety. But somewhere between "let's be thoughtful" and "let's add another approval layer," we cross an invisible line.

The moment that committee joke landed, something shifted. For the first time, people acknowledged the absurdity out loud. Not with cynicism, but with relief. As though someone had finally named the elephant that had been sitting in every video conference for six months.

That honesty became our opening.

How Silos Are Born

Here's what I've learned about silos: they don't begin with bad intent. They begin with focus.

When organizations are small, everyone does a bit of everything. It's chaotic, but it works because everyone sees the whole picture. Then growth happens. And with growth comes specialization, marketing handles customers, finance handles numbers, operations handles delivery, HR handles culture. Each function builds deep expertise.

At first, it's beautiful. Focus brings efficiency. Boundaries bring accountability. But efficiency carries a quiet cost that compounds over time: it teaches teams to optimize for themselves.

Each function begins creating its own playbook, its own language, even its own heroes. Marketing celebrates creativity; finance celebrates control. IT prizes precision; HR prizes empathy. These values aren't wrong, they're just incomplete when they exist in isolation.

Over time, what started as a division of labor becomes division of logic. Instead of working toward the same mission, functions start protecting their version of success.

If you listen carefully inside a large organization, you can hear its sociology at work:

"We in sales…"

"They in finance…"

Each sentence draws a subtle boundary between who belongs and who doesn't. It reflects in-group bias, our instinct to trust people like us and doubt those who aren't. In organizations, that bias becomes a performance tax.

When teams no longer trust each other's intent, they add layers of validation to compensate, extra reports, extra reviews, extra meetings. That's how a simple approval process morphs into seventeen signatures. Trust gets replaced by templates.

Silos also persist because they create an illusion of control. If my department owns a process, I can manage its risk, shape its narrative, protect its reputation. Sharing control feels like sharing vulnerability.

But the tighter the control, the smaller the impact. Leaders defend turf instead of discovering opportunities.

Chapter 12
From Silos to Pods

History gave silos legitimacy. Frederick Taylor's Scientific Management divided work into measurable units. But it also built invisible fences around knowledge.

What worked for manufacturing doesn't work for modern collaboration. Today's value comes from combining ideas faster. But many leaders still manage like factory foremen, believing coordination slows output when disconnection is the real drag.

Markets now move faster than org charts can adapt. Customers expect seamless experiences, marketing, product, finance, and service all acting as one. But inside most companies, those functions sit on different floors, use different metrics, and meet only during escalations.

The world is networked; organizations remain linear. That gap kills opportunity.

The Breakthrough That Changed Everything

Back in that steering committee meeting, with twelve functions represented and zero forward momentum, I decided to ask a different question.

"If you had to build a small team to actually make this work," I said, "not to review it, not to sign off on it, but to own it end-to-end—who would you pick?"

Silence. Then, slowly, names emerged.

Not titles. Not departments. Names of people who understood both the business problem and the technical constraints. People who could make decisions without escalating every choice to committee. The list had six names.

That day, the organization's first pod was born. Accidentally. Out of frustration more than strategy.

They didn't have a formal charter or new titles or rebranded business cards. What they had was clarity, accountability, and permission to move. Within eight weeks, that small cross-functional team achieved what seventeen sign-offs couldn't deliver in six months.

They didn't dismantle the organization overnight. They simply ignored its walls long enough to prove what was possible when connection replaced caution.

The lesson: Silos are not structures—they're stories. Stories that begin with good logic and end with lost momentum. Breaking them isn't an act of rebellion; it's an act of renewal.

What Pods Actually Are

When organizations finally admit that silos are slowing them down, the instinctive response is predictable: launch a "collaboration initiative." There will be town halls, task forces, and new dashboards. But six months later, everyone quietly slips back into the old rhythm.

Collaboration can't be mandated. It has to be designed.

A pod is a small, cross-functional team built around a single outcome, not a department, not a project, but an outcome. It includes all the capabilities needed to deliver that outcome end-to-end, with minimal dependence on other functions.

If a traditional org chart is a vertical hierarchy of expertise, a pod is a horizontal circle of accountability.

A typical pod might bring together a product manager, a finance analyst, an engineer, and a marketing lead. Each brings deep expertise, but they share one collective metric that defines success. They make decisions together, learn together, and win or lose together.

Chapter 12
From Silos to Pods

Pods aren't new. They're simply formalizing what the best small teams have always done, stay close to the problem and to each other.

The Shift from Silos to Pods

Siloed Organizations	Pod-based Organizations
Decisions climb hierarchy for approval	Decisions made where work happens
Responsibility distributed widely	Ownership concentrated clearly
Teams optimize for their department	Teams optimize for shared outcome
Multiple sign-offs create delays	One conversation, immediate context
Link between effort and impact diluted	Directed link between effort and outcome
People wait for permission	People act from ownership

Hierarchy pushes decisions upward, distributes responsibility widely, and encourages teams to optimize locally. The result is delay, diluted accountability, and a weak connection between effort and impact. Ownership-driven systems work differently. Decisions sit close to the work, responsibility is clear, context is immediate, and teams optimize for the outcome that matters. People don't wait to be told what to do. They act because they own the result.

How the Best Organizations Made Pods Work

When I study organizations that successfully transitioned from silos to pods, three companies keep surfacing with patterns worth stealing.

Spotify: The Squad That Changed Music

Spotify didn't invent pods, but they popularized them under the name 'squads,' small autonomous teams that own one part of the user experience end to end. Each squad has its own backlog, its own rituals, and the authority to ship features without waiting for cross-functional approval.

What made Spotify's model work wasn't just the structure, it was the philosophy behind it. Product manager Henrik Kniberg, who documented Spotify's approach, emphasized that squads needed to be "loosely coupled but tightly aligned." They could move independently because everyone understood the broader mission.

The results spoke clearly: Spotify went from deploying code every few weeks to deploying multiple times per day. Decision-making cycles that used to take months collapsed to days. Not because they worked harder, but because they removed the coordination tax between specialized functions.

By 2016, Spotify had organized its entire 1,600-person engineering organization into squads, grouped into "tribes" (collections of squads working on related areas) and supported by "guilds" (communities of practice that shared knowledge across squads). The model wasn't perfect, and it has since evolved, but it proved that large organizations could operate with startup speed when they designed for connection.

Chapter 12
From Silos to Pods

Amazon: The Two-Pizza Rule

Jeff Bezos famously instituted the "two-pizza team" rule at Amazon: if a team can't be fed with two pizzas, it's too big. The logic was simple but radical, small teams move fast because communication stays human.

What's less known is how Amazon backed up that rule with real authority. These weren't just small teams; they were small teams with genuine ownership. Each had its own P&L, its own key metrics, and the power to make decisions without escalation. They operated like micro-businesses within the larger company.

Research from MIT Sloan Management Review studied Amazon's approach and found that decision-making speed increased by 40% when teams operated this way. But the more interesting finding was cultural: teams reported higher engagement, lower burnout, and greater pride in their work because the link between effort and outcome was finally visible again.

Amazon's model taught me something crucial: pods work not just because they're small, but because they're empowered. Authority without ownership is paralysis. Ownership without authority is theater.

Haier: The Factory That Became 4,000 Startups

If you think pods only work in tech companies, consider Haier, the Chinese appliance manufacturer that transformed its 70,000-person workforce into more than 4,000 micro-enterprises.

CEO Zhang Ruimin didn't just reorganize the company; he reimagined it. Each micro-enterprise operates like a startup within Haier, with its own customers (internal or external), its own profit-and-loss statement, and the authority to make decisions about products, pricing, and partnerships.

Lead Less, Build More

The transformation wasn't easy—it took nearly a decade. But the results were remarkable. According to Harvard Business Review's analysis, Haier's revenue per employee increased by 180% between 2007 and 2019, even as the company reduced layers of management from 12 to just 3.

What Haier proved is that the pod model isn't just for knowledge work or software development. It works anywhere you have smart people solving problems that require cross-functional coordination. The moment you remove the coordination tax, performance unlocks.

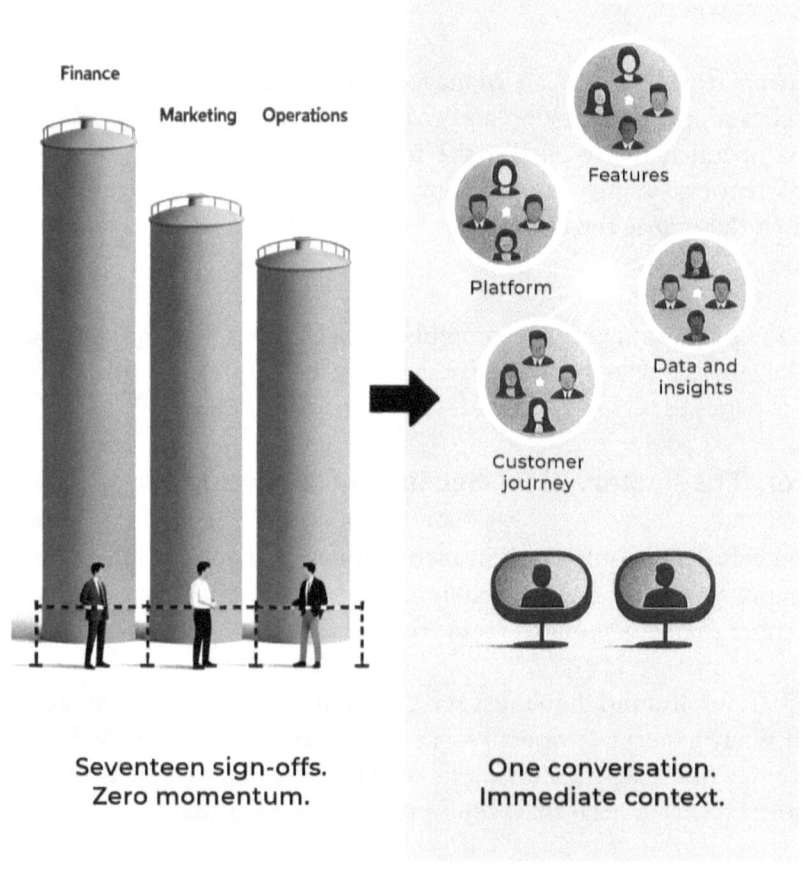

Chapter 12
From Silos to Pods

Designing Pods That Actually Work

It's easy to draw circles on a whiteboard and call them pods. The hard part is making those circles work when budgets tighten, priorities collide, and the old hierarchy quietly returns to reclaim territory.

I've learned that designing pods isn't about rearranging reporting lines—it's about re-engineering how work travels through the organization. Who decides. Who learns. How accountability moves.

Let me share what I've seen work.

Start by Mapping Dependencies

Every organization thinks its structure is the problem. More often, it's the handoffs between structures that slow things down.

During a finance transformation I supported, we began by mapping every process end-to-end across regions. On paper, there were five core functions. In practice, there were 28 handoffs for a single customer transaction. When teams saw the map, no one argued for more alignment meetings. They simply asked: "Can we make this path shorter?"

Pods do exactly that, they collapse the distance between cause and effect by bringing everyone who matters to an outcome into one space. Mapping dependencies doesn't just reveal inefficiency; it exposes opportunity. Every redundant interface is a candidate for a pod.

Define One North Star Metric

Silos distribute responsibility widely; pods concentrate it clearly.

Each pod should own one North Star metric, the single outcome it exists to deliver. A customer-experience pod might own "onboarding time." A finance pod might own "forecast accuracy." A supply-chain pod might own "fulfillment cost per order."

When ownership is clear, accountability becomes collective, not political. People stop optimizing for their department's scorecard and start optimizing for the pod's mission.

I watched a global technology client reorganize 120 people into 15 pods, each owning a measurable business metric. Within six months, decision time for new initiatives dropped from 45 days to 10. Not because people worked harder, because they finally knew what "winning" meant.

Build Connector Roles

Even the best pods need connective tissue, people who translate across domains and prevent local optimization from drifting into fragmentation.

These aren't middle managers rebadged; they're context architects. Their job is to ensure pods learn from each other, share patterns, and align on purpose without losing autonomy.

During a global finance transformation at reputed firm, we used connector roles extensively. Regional pods worked independently on client accounts, but connectors ensured that automation learnings from one geography benefited others. The structure allowed for autonomy without fragmentation, many hands, one mind.

Rotate and Refresh Membership

Pods thrive on diversity of perspective, but keeping the same composition for too long breeds familiarity. And familiarity breeds comfort, which eventually breeds blindness to new possibilities.

High-performing organizations deliberately rotate pod members every six to twelve months. This practice spreads context and builds empathy. When you've sat in another pod's seat, you stop saying "they don't understand" and start saying "let me help."

Rotation doesn't just share knowledge, it shares ownership of culture.

Equip Pods for Learning

Pods are built to move fast, but speed without learning is just motion. Each pod should operate with a learning rhythm, a weekly retrospective asking three questions: What surprised us? What slowed us? What will we do differently?

In one client organization, this simple ritual reduced repeated errors by 40% in three months. Micro-reflections prevent autopilot.

The Psychology of Connection

You can design perfect structures and assign clear metrics, but if people don't feel safe to speak, share, and stretch, the structure becomes theater. Pods work only when culture catches up with design.

Every pod begins with a small leap of faith—faith that others will deliver, that decisions will be fair, that intentions are aligned. That trust isn't declared in kick-off meetings; it's earned through visibility.

At a technology client that reorganized into pods, we asked team members how they would know if trust was growing. One engineer gave us the best answer: **"When I stop cc-ing everyone just to be safe."**

That became our metric. Fewer copied emails. Shorter meetings. More direct conversations. Trust made visible through behavior.

Harvard professor Amy Edmondson has spent decades studying what she calls psychological safety, the belief that you can speak up, admit mistakes, or challenge ideas without fear of embarrassment or retribution. Her research shows that teams with high psychological safety outperform others, even when they make more errors initially. Why? Because they learn faster.

Safety isn't about comfort, it's about candor. And candor is what transforms a group of individuals into a genuine team.

Transitioning from silos to pods triggers three predictable fears that leaders must name out loud:

Loss of control. Managers fear invisibility when decisions decentralize.

Loss of expertise. Specialists worry that cross-functional collaboration will dilute depth.

Loss of identity. Departments built around legacy pride fear irrelevance.

Each of these fears is human. Ignoring them is managerial arrogance.

During a leadership offsite for a manufacturing company, one senior manager confessed: "I'm scared of not being the expert anymore." The CEO's response was perfect: "You'll still be the expert, just surrounded by others whose expertise makes yours more powerful."

That reframing turned fear into partnership.

Pods also need rituals, small, consistent practices that reinforce connection. Daily stand-ups to share progress and blockers. Demo days to showcase what was learned, not just what was launched. Retrospectives where teams reflect honestly on what worked and what didn't, with no blame, only learning.

These rituals build rhythm, and rhythm builds belonging.

Chapter 12
From Silos to Pods

At Airbnb and IDEO, "show-and-tell" sessions let teams present prototypes to peers, celebrate creative risks, and normalize failure as tuition. "Nothing builds trust like watching another team's demo fail gracefully."

Pods don't need lavish offsites to build culture. They need shared truth told regularly.

What Leaders Must Do Differently

When organizations move from silos to pods, leaders have to reimagine what it means to manage. It's less about directing traffic and more about designing flow.

Pods thrive when leaders act as architects of connection—orchestrating trust, clarity, and alignment across teams without suffocating their autonomy.

Play Architect, Not Manager

Managers maintain systems, while architects shape them. In a pod world, the role shifts from approving decisions to creating an environment that produces good ones.

Architects design clarity: clear goals, clear boundaries, and clear access to resources. They also design space, psychological and operational—for experimentation. And they replace traditional governance with rapid feedback loops.

At one client, leadership replaced monthly steering committees with weekly "pulse" meetings. Each pod presented three slides: what we accomplished this week, what decision we need next, what help we require. No status theater. No 60-page decks. Leaders realized their job was not to inspect but to unblock.

A leader's real measure becomes: "How many smart decisions happen without me?" The more your teams act confidently within intent, the stronger your architecture is.

Frame Problems as Shared Missions

Silos define problems by function: "Finance needs better forecasting." "Operations needs efficiency." Pods frame problems by outcome: "We need to deliver faster, smarter, and together."

When you reframe issues as shared missions, you change who feels responsible. At one client, we reframed "reduce costs" as "free capacity for innovation." Suddenly conversations shifted from cuts to creativity. Everyone found ownership because everyone saw gain.

Language creates ownership; ownership creates movement.

Protect Time for Connection

Pods move fast, which means connection can quietly erode under pressure. Leaders must guard space for reflection, weekly huddles, cross-pod check-ins, learning demos. These moments aren't overhead; they're oxygen.

When teams pause to exchange insights, they multiply learning and prevent duplication. A 30-minute conversation can save 30 days of rework. Leaders who see conversation as cost end up paying for silence later.

Reward Collaboration, Not Just Results

Most appraisal systems reward what gets delivered, not how. In a networked model, how is half the value.

We began recognizing people who contributed to others' success. That included mentoring across pods, sharing code, or coaching peers. At one global client, this took the form of 'collaboration credits,' nominations for individuals who helped another team move forward.

What leaders celebrate becomes culture.

Model the Behavior You Expect

If leaders hoard information, teams will too. If leaders admit mistakes publicly, teams will take smart risks. Culture cascades from conduct, not communication.

In one transformation I supported, the CEO began every all-hands with a segment called "What I Got Wrong This Month." It wasn't theatre, it was permission. Teams soon started opening meetings the same way. Transparency spread faster than any process document could manage.

Leadership vulnerability creates organizational strength.

Two Companies, Two Paths

The contrast between silos and pods isn't theoretical, it's visceral. You can see it in the mood of meetings, the speed of decisions, the energy of teams. Let me share two stories that show the difference.

The Matrix That Froze

A global consumer company launched an ambitious data-analytics initiative across product lines and geographies. "One source of truth," the CEO announced at the kick-off.

By month three, that truth had seventeen interpretations.

Every region wanted custom dashboards. IT demanded standardized templates. Marketing insisted on design freedom. Finance wanted control of the KPIs. Six steering committees and no steering.

Meetings became rituals of delay—each function waiting for others to agree. People stopped asking "What's right for the company?" and started asking "Whose sign-off do we still need?"

The breakthrough came from exhaustion. A mid-level manager decided to form a "task pod" of volunteers, one analyst, one finance manager, one marketer, one developer. They weren't authorized; they were just tired of waiting.

They built a prototype dashboard in two weeks. It wasn't perfect, but it worked. Within a month, executives were using it. When the project went global, the task pod became the template.

What bureaucracy delayed for six months, one self-formed pod achieved in 40 days. Once people saw progress, the walls began to crack.

The Pod That Scaled

A logistics company I advised wanted to improve on-time deliveries across 30 countries. Historically, operations, planning, and technology worked separately. Each blamed the others when delays occurred.

Instead of adding another coordination layer, the COO decided to pilot a delivery pod, one cross-functional team with end-to-end responsibility for a single shipping lane. It included representatives from every function involved in delivery, each with real authority.

The pod met daily, shared one KPI, on-time rate—and could make any decision within its scope. Within eight weeks, on-time performance improved by 18%.

But the more profound change was cultural. People stopped using the phrase "our department" and started saying "our lane." Data scientists sat with truck planners. Customer-service agents joined operations huddles. The silos didn't disappear, they became translucent.

Chapter 12
From Silos to Pods

One employee summed it up beautifully: "Before, we delivered parcels. Now, we deliver promises."

That line captured the essence of connection. When people feel collective ownership of purpose, accountability becomes shared joy, not shared burden.

What This Means for You

Every organization starts with connection and ends with complexity. In the early days, everyone knows everyone; ideas move faster than approvals. But as success grows, so does structure. What began as coordination becomes control.

Silos were never the enemy—they were simply yesterday's answer to yesterday's problems. They made sense when work was linear and predictable. But the world today is neither.

The challenge of leadership now isn't managing size, it's restoring flow. Helping people feel connected to purpose, to one another, and to outcomes that matter.

Pods are not an alternative to structure. They're a reminder of what structure was always meant to do: amplify collaboration, not replace it.

When I reflect on transformations I've witnessed, one truth stands out: people rarely resist change; they resist isolation. When you give them shared purpose, clarity of ownership, and a trusted circle to build with, they rediscover energy that hierarchy had quietly drained.

Moving from silos to pods is not an organizational redesign, it's a cultural awakening. A shift from managing compliance to enabling commitment. It requires humility from leaders who once found power in control and now must find it in connection. It asks teams to replace "my function" with "our mission."

The walls we built for efficiency will not save us in an age that rewards empathy and agility. The bridges we build now will.

Where to Start

If you're ready to experiment with pods in your organization, here's how to begin:

Identify one cross-functional process to "podify." Don't boil the ocean. Pick a single outcome that matters, customer onboarding, product launch, cost reduction. Create a small team with all skills needed to own that outcome end-to-end. Give them authority for 90 days and watch what happens.

Define one North Star metric. Make it measurable. Make it meaningful. Make sure every member of the pod can influence it directly. Review it weekly, together.

Hold a bi-weekly demo day. Share what the pod learned, not just what it delivered. When other teams see transparency, they'll want in.

Rotate one member every quarter. When people understand each other's challenges, silos lose their grip.

Publish wins publicly. Celebrate not just results, but the collaboration that produced them. Recognition shapes behavior.

The future doesn't belong to organizations that know the most. It belongs to those that connect the fastest—where information flows without fear and people act without waiting for permission.

Because in the end, progress isn't made by structures. It's made by small groups of connected people who decide that silos will not define them anymore.

Chapter 13
Change That Sticks

The Initiative That Faded

At its peak, Nokia was untouchable.

In 2007, it owned more than 40 percent of the global mobile-phone market. Its brand stood for reliability, innovation, and Nordic discipline. Inside headquarters in Espoo, executives spoke confidently about "the next transformation." They held town halls, hired consultants, and produced slide decks forecasting the shift to the smartphone era.

Everything about the transformation looked textbook perfect.

Except that it didn't work.

By 2013, Nokia had lost 90 percent of its market value and was forced to sell its handset business to Microsoft. When researchers later studied the failure, they found no shortage of strategy, intelligence, or effort. What they found was fear , a culture so conditioned by its own success that people hesitated to tell uncomfortable truths.

Managers who saw early warning signs of Apple's iPhone hesitated to speak up. Middle leaders quietly admitted they doubted the new direction but waited for consensus from above. Everyone was changing in presentations. No one was changing in behavior.

One engineer described it best: "We were always transforming. We just weren't actually changing."

The programs were bold. The PowerPoints beautiful. The belief fragile.

Nokia's story isn't a failure of intelligence. It's a failure of reinforcement. Change was launched, not lived. The new behaviors never repeated long enough to overwrite the old ones.

The Contrast That Teaches

Seven years later, Microsoft was standing at a similar crossroads.

Profitable, powerful, but trapped inside a culture of competition and control. Engineers spoke of "Windows vs. Office," not "Microsoft." The company was winning quarters but losing spirit.

When Satya Nadella became CEO in 2014, he didn't start with reorganization charts. He started with a conversation. His message was almost spiritual in its simplicity: adopt a growth mindset. It wasn't a new process or tool. It was a new story about learning.

Meetings began to change.

Instead of defending positions, people started asking questions. Performance reviews shifted from "prove you're right" to "show what you learned." Leaders modeled vulnerability by sharing what they got wrong.

Within five years, Microsoft's market value quadrupled. But more importantly, the company rediscovered its curiosity.

The Lesson Beneath Both

Two companies. Two transformations. Two outcomes.

Nokia tried to transform by telling people what to change. Microsoft transformed by teaching people how to keep changing.

That's the difference between momentum and memory.

Momentum launches change. Memory sustains it.

I've watched this pattern repeat across organizations for years. Change begins with conviction, but it survives only through consistency. The problem isn't resistance, it's reversion. People don't cling to the past because they dislike the future. They cling to it because it's familiar, rewarded, and safe.

Transformation requires moving from heroic leadership to building systems. This chapter extends that principle: change sticks when it's embedded in systems of reinforcement, not dependent on leaders pushing it forward.

Transformation fails when leaders mistake an event for evolution. They treat the kick-off as victory instead of the starting gun.

Real change doesn't collapse in the announcement. It collapses in the afterlife, in the quiet weeks when energy fades and the new way hasn't yet become muscle memory.

That's what this chapter is about.

How to turn movement into memory. How to make the future strong enough to resist the gravitational pull of the past.

Because change doesn't stick by decree. It sticks by design.

And as I've learned the hard way, the work of change begins the moment the spotlight ends.

Why Change Fades

Every organization begins change with good intent.

There are workshops, slogans, dashboards, and leaders who declare, "This time will be different."

But after the spotlight fades, something predictable happens. People return quietly to the familiar. The new tools are still there, the new slides still circulate, but the old habits start slipping back like gravity.

Within a year, the transformation becomes another corporate ghost, remembered in case studies, not lived in meetings.

Why does this happen so consistently?

Chapter 13
Change That Sticks

1. Fatigue — The Weight of Constant Transformation

Most organizations are not short of change. They are exhausted by it.

Every year brings a new initiative, each promising renewal but demanding attention from the same limited pool of energy. When everything is "strategic," nothing feels sustainable.

Employees don't resist change. They ration it.

They participate selectively, preserving just enough energy to survive the next wave.

McKinsey's long-running research on transformation success rates shows that over 70 percent of major change programs fail to sustain results beyond 18 months. Fatigue is one of the most cited causes.

Change, like physical training, needs rest between repetitions. Without recovery, enthusiasm turns into erosion.

2. Forgetting — Habits That Don't Stick

Change doesn't fade in meetings. It fades in mornings.

It fades in the first week after launch when the old inbox routines, approval processes, and informal shortcuts reappear.

Most organizations underestimate how deeply habits are embedded. Culture is not what leaders say. It's what teams repeat without thinking.

Unless new behaviors are reinforced long enough to replace old reflexes, the system reverts by default.

That's why every transformation needs reinforcement rituals and visible, consistent behaviors that keep the new alive until it becomes normal.

If trust is the operating system, repetition is the software patch.

3. Fragmentation — Change Without Connection

Even when momentum begins, it rarely moves evenly.

Departments interpret transformation through their own lenses — finance sees it as discipline, HR as culture, technology as efficiency. Soon, the enterprise ends up with many versions of "change," each optimized locally, none integrated globally.

It's like tuning every instrument separately and wondering why the orchestra sounds off-key.

Fragmentation also happens when success metrics diverge. One function measures output, another measures experience, and soon the energy that began collectively becomes competitive.

Change sticks when people see the same goal from different angles, not different goals from the same slogan.

4. Leadership Turnover — When Ownership Moves On

Another silent killer of change is time.

The leaders who start the movement often don't stay to finish it. Successors, even when well-intentioned, want to leave their mark — a new framework, a fresh slogan, a different consultant.

Continuity gets traded for novelty.

One global company I advised had launched a purpose-driven culture transformation that gained real traction. Then the leadership changed, and the new team quietly renamed it "Version 2.0." Within months, employees began joking: "Every two years, we get a new purpose."

Nothing erodes belief faster than seeing leadership move on while asking others to stay committed.

5. Measurement Myopia — Tracking Output, Ignoring Energy

Organizations love numbers, but not all numbers matter equally.

Most organizations track what's easy, such as training hours, process adoption, and cost savings, but rarely measure belief energy, the intangible pulse of commitment.

Change is emotional before it's operational.

When pride, curiosity, and hope go unmeasured, leaders miss the early signs of fatigue and disillusionment. You can't spreadsheet belief, but you can see it in behavior: participation rates, proactive ideas, tone in meetings.

As Peter Drucker once observed, "Culture eats strategy for breakfast." But culture, left unmeasured, often starves to death quietly.

The Underlying Pattern

All these reasons, fatigue, forgetting, fragmentation, turnover, and myopic measurement, share a common thread.

Leaders stop reinforcing the new before it becomes natural.

Change fades not because people are weak, but because reinforcement is weaker than routine.

Transformation is not a single event. It's a sustained conversation.

The problem is that most leaders leave the room before the conversation is finished.

The Four Anchors of Sticky Change

Change, at its heart, is an act of psychology before it becomes a process.

It sticks when belief outlives the announcement.

Over years of watching transformations rise and fade, I've come to see four consistent anchors that determine whether change becomes permanent: Clarity, Capability, Community, and Cadence.

If even one is missing, momentum slips away.

These anchors are simple, but they aren't easy. They demand consistency long after enthusiasm fades.

1. Clarity — The Compass That Points to "Why"

People rarely resist what they understand. They resist what they don't feel connected to.

Every change starts with a story — but most organizations rush past the storytelling stage. They tell people what's changing and how it will happen, but not why it matters to them.

Leaders overestimate communication and underestimate meaning.

In one organization I worked with, the CFO opened a digital transformation kick-off with charts about productivity and automation. Employees nodded politely but looked uneasy. A week later, he reframed the message:

Chapter 13
Change That Sticks

> *"We're not automating to remove people. We're automating to remove the parts of your job that keep you from thinking."*

That single sentence changed the room.

Clarity isn't repetition of facts. It's alignment of purpose.

People follow leaders who can make complexity feel clear and change feel personal.

Leader Moves:

- Start every major communication with the "why," even if people have heard it before
- Translate the organization's ambition into individual relevance
- Replace jargon with emotion — "Efficiency" doesn't inspire; "freeing time for creativity" does

2. Capability — The Bridge Between Aspiration and Action

No change sticks if people aren't equipped to live it.

Organizations often announce transformations with bold intent but forget that new behaviors require new skills. Capability is the bridge between aspiration and reality.

A finance team I once coached was asked to move from reporting to analytics, from describing the past to anticipating the future. Initially, anxiety ran high. "We're accountants, not data scientists," someone said.

So we built small capability pods. They learned visualization tools, storytelling with data, and critical thinking. Within months, they began presenting insights, not just numbers.

One analyst told me, "Earlier, I used to prepare slides. Now I prepare stories."

Capability transforms fear into confidence. It tells people, "You're not being replaced. You're being upgraded."

Leader Moves:

- Audit the new skills change demands: technical, behavioral and emotional
- Invest visibly in learning, time, not just money
- Celebrate first learners as loudly as first adopters

3. Community — The Network That Sustains Belief

Change sticks when belief becomes social.

Formal sponsors may launch transformation, but informal networks sustain it. People copy peers, not posters.

At one technology firm, a group of early adopters of a new collaboration tool started helping others without being asked. They became the "quiet champions." Within months, adoption tripled, not because of corporate mandates, but because employees trusted those like them.

Community creates peer accountability. It turns change from a corporate message into a human movement.

The most successful transformations I've seen always have an inner circle of believers who lead from within, volunteers who prove the change works and make it emotionally safe for others to join.

As Margaret Mead once wrote, "Never doubt that a small group of thoughtful, committed citizens can change the world."

Chapter 13
Change That Sticks

Inside companies, that group is your community.

Leader Moves:

- Identify early believers and empower them as "change sherpas"
- Create platforms where success stories travel horizontally, not just top-down
- Reward collaboration over compliance

4. Cadence — The Rhythm That Keeps Change Alive

Momentum dies when the rhythm of reinforcement stops.

Most organizations treat change like a campaign , intensive at the start, silent afterward. But culture changes not through events, but through rituals.

Cadence is how you turn intention into habit, through regular meetings, reviews, and reflections that remind people what matters.

A global firm I worked with replaced its monthly "status review" with a "learning review." Each team shared one thing they improved, one thing they struggled with, and one idea they wanted to test. Within months, the tone of meetings shifted from fear to curiosity.

Cadence isn't about frequency. It's about predictability. People trust what they can count on.

Just as heartbeat rhythm keeps life going, review rhythm keeps change alive.

Leader Moves:

- Establish recurring rituals: learning reviews, storytelling sessions, quarterly reflection forums

- Measure consistency before results
- Publicly recognize persistence by acknowledging those who show up and sustain effort long after the buzz has faded.

The Four Anchors Together

Clarity gives direction. Capability gives confidence. Community gives belonging. Cadence gives durability.

Together, they turn transformation from a sprint into a marathon.

When leaders commit to these four anchors, they stop managing change as a project and start nurturing it as a living organism.

Because in the end, change doesn't stick by decree or design alone.

It sticks when people understand it, can do it, feel supported in it, and keep doing it long enough to forget it was ever new.

From Rollout to Ritual

Most organizations are world-class at rolling out change.

They design glossy launch decks, town halls, and detailed communication plans. They print banners, commission videos, and schedule milestones.

And then, quietly, everything fades.

Because rollout is an event. Ritual is a system.

Rollouts announce intention. Rituals reinforce behavior.

The difference between transformation that sparks and transformation that sticks is simple: rituals.

Chapter 13
Change That Sticks

The Launch Illusion

Every major transformation starts with high energy. Leadership visibility is at its peak. Budgets flow. Consultants arrive.

But the launch phase creates a dangerous illusion that enthusiasm equals change.

When the initial buzz fades, the system seeks equilibrium. Without reinforcement, old behaviors reassert themselves because they're easier and familiar.

The launch wins hearts. The ritual wins habits.

I once observed a multinational that had invested heavily in customer-centricity. Posters shouted "Customer First!" across offices. But in meetings, metrics still prioritized internal cost targets. Employees joked, "Customer first — after finance."

The company had rolled out a message. It hadn't ritualized a mindset.

The Power of Keystone Habits

Sustainable change doesn't require hundreds of new behaviors. It requires a few powerful ones practiced consistently.

In his research on habit formation, Charles Duhigg calls them "keystone habits." These are small actions that trigger broader transformation.

In organizations, keystone habits might include:

- Starting meetings with a story about customer impact
- Ending every project review with one lesson learned
- Replacing "status updates" with "learning updates"

When these actions repeat predictably, they build rhythm, and rhythm builds belief.

Think of rituals as emotional muscle memory. They remind people who they are and what they value.

Microsoft's Growth Mindset

One of the most enduring examples of transformation through ritual comes from Microsoft.

When Satya Nadella introduced the idea of a growth mindset, it wasn't a one-time campaign. It became embedded in daily vocabulary and systems.

Performance reviews started rewarding curiosity and collaboration. Leaders began sharing personal stories of learning failures. Recruitment interviews included questions that assessed learning agility.

Within a few years, "What did you learn?" became the company's cultural heartbeat.

That's how ideas turn into identity, when they show up in how people talk, decide, and celebrate..

Singapore's SkillsFuture

Singapore's SkillsFuture initiative offers a national example of change as ritual.

Rather than treating reskilling as a one-time policy, the government embedded continuous learning into civic life. Every citizen receives learning credits, and training is normalized as an ongoing rhythm, not an event for crisis.

Chapter 13
Change That Sticks

By turning reskilling into a national habit, Singapore ensured adaptability wasn't reactive, it was routine.

The lesson for organizations is clear: when learning becomes rhythm, adaptability becomes reflex.

Designing Rituals That Stick

Rituals need three qualities to endure:

Simplicity — They should be easy enough to do even on bad days
Visibility — Everyone should know when they're happening and why
Meaning — They must connect to purpose, not process

A financial institution I worked with replaced its monthly "compliance check-in" with a 15-minute "integrity huddle." The content didn't change, but the language did. The tone shifted from inspection to pride. Attendance went up. So did engagement.

Rituals don't have to be grand. They just have to be grounded.

When Rituals Replace Reminders

A leader once asked me, "How will I know when this transformation has truly stuck?"

My answer: "When you stop reminding people, and they start reminding you."

That's the moment change becomes self-sustaining.

When employees quote the new principles unprompted. When managers enforce them without escalation. When the organization polices itself through pride, not policy.

That's when rollout graduates to ritual.

Rituals are not mechanical repetition. They are emotional reinforcement. They tell people, "This is who we are now."

Change feels fragile until rituals take root.

Then it feels inevitable.

The Neuroscience of Habit Change

Leaders often talk about 'embedding change,' but what they really mean, whether they realize it or not, is rewiring behavior.

Change sticks when the brain stops seeing it as new.

Neuroscience tells us that every habit — personal or organizational — follows the same three-step loop: Cue → Routine → Reward. Charles Duhigg popularized this model in The Power of Habit, showing that the basal ganglia stores repetitive behavior patterns. The brain reinforces whatever pattern gets repeated and rewarded, which is why old organizational habits are so persistent — they're stored in muscle memory, not slides or systems.

The Cue: What Starts the Pattern

Every behavior begins with a cue — a signal that tells people, "Do the usual thing now."

In organizations, cues are everywhere:

- A calendar invite that says "weekly status meeting"
- A report that triggers debate about variance, not insight
- A boss's silence when someone challenges tradition

Chapter 13
Change That Sticks

If the cues of the old culture remain untouched, new behavior never has a chance.

When I work with teams on transformation, I often start by asking: "What tells you that the old way is still alive?" Their answers are remarkably consistent, pointing to templates, meeting agendas, approval chains, and even room layouts.

Changing cues is more powerful than changing speeches.

You can't talk people out of a habit. You have to interrupt the pattern.

Leader Moves:

- Audit recurring cues by asking what in your calendar or processes still signal the past
- Replace one ritualistic cue with a new one — instead of Monday "status calls," hold Monday "learning calls"
- Small changes in cues trigger large shifts in behavior

The Routine: What Gets Repeated

The brain conserves energy by running known routines automatically.

That's why transformation fatigue sets in, people are being asked to consciously manage what used to be automatic.

The trick is to shorten the time between awareness and new action.

When Singapore's SkillsFuture initiative encouraged citizens to take short learning modules, it was leveraging this principle — make the new behavior small enough to repeat without friction. In companies, that means lowering barriers: shorter forms, faster approvals, quicker feedback loops.

Habits don't stick because they're big. They stick because they're doable.

Leader Moves:

- Design "micro-behaviors" instead of mandates
- Encourage teams to experiment daily, not quarterly
- Reinforce consistency over intensity —it's better to do a new behavior 20 times imperfectly than 2 times perfectly

The Reward: Why the Brain Keeps Coming Back

No habit lasts without an emotional payoff.

Rewards tell the brain, "This loop is worth saving."

In organizations, rewards are often delayed or disconnected from effort, with bonuses paid once a year and recognition buried in metrics. But the brain learns through immediacy.

Harvard research on behavior reinforcement shows that visible, near-term rewards double the likelihood of habit retention. That's why agile teams celebrate 'sprint wins,' because small, frequent moments of recognition keep motivation alive.

The most powerful reward, though, is meaning.

When people feel that their work matters, the brain releases dopamine, the same chemical associated with satisfaction after achievement.

Meaning is the long-term currency of habit.

Leader Moves:

- Build emotional reward into change by publicly appreciating effort, not just results.
- Use storytelling to connect daily actions to larger purpose

- Replace performance dashboards with progress dashboards that show learning, not just numbers

Why This Matters

Habits are the brain's way of saving energy. Culture is the organization's way of doing the same.

To change either, you must change the loop: alter the cue, redesign the routine, and make the reward immediate and meaningful.

When leaders manage that loop consistently, change stops being a fight against memory and becomes an upgrade to it.

Transformation then feels less like forcing people to think differently and more like helping them remember who they always wanted to be.

Because in the end, sustainable change isn't about new rules. It's about new reflexes.

The Sustainability Loop

Transformation fails when it's treated like a marathon run at sprint speed.

Organizations push hard, make progress, and then collapse under their own momentum.

Sustained change isn't about going faster. It's about learning how to loop by sensing when to adjust, simplifying when complexity creeps in, sustaining what matters, and scaling only when the new way is stable.

Every enduring transformation I've seen follows this quiet four-step rhythm: Sense → Simplify → Sustain → Scale.

1. Sense — Listen Before You Push

The most adaptive organizations don't manage change. They monitor it.

By noticing early signs of fatigue, confusion, or misplaced enthusiasm, they prevent problems from becoming failures.

Sensing means staying curious even after the rollout is "done."

A global consumer firm I worked with created a "change pulse" — a three-question monthly survey sent to all teams:

- What's working?
- What's tiring you?
- What do you need next?

It took two minutes to complete and gave leadership priceless insight. One quarter, the most common word in responses was "meetings." They realized people weren't resisting the change. They were drowning in updates.

The company cut meeting time by 30%, and energy rebounded.

Listening is not a soft skill. It's a survival skill.

Leader Moves:

- Keep small feedback channels open long after launch
- Pay attention to emotional data as much as operational data
- When energy dips, don't escalate pressure; increase empathy.

2. Simplify — Complexity Kills Consistency

Every new change adds processes, metrics, and governance layers — until people forget why they started.

Chapter 13
Change That Sticks

Simplicity isn't laziness. It's precision. It keeps people's attention on impact instead of instruction.

Toyota has a rule: every new initiative must make someone's job simpler, not harder. If it doesn't, the change is reworked.

In one finance transformation I led, we realized 40% of our process controls existed mainly to ensure other controls worked. We removed redundancy, documented the essentials, and suddenly progress accelerated.

Simplification is subtraction with intent. It doesn't reduce ambition. It removes friction.

Leader Moves:

- Audit all new processes added during transformation
- Eliminate anything that doesn't directly serve the customer or employee experience
- Teach leaders to value clarity over comprehensiveness. When people can remember what matters, they can repeat it

3. Sustain — Protect the Rituals

Sustainability isn't continuity. It's maintenance with meaning.

Organizations often let maintenance slip because novelty feels more rewarding. But lasting change depends on protecting the rituals that keep belief alive.

In one client organization, quarterly "learning reviews" were introduced during a transformation. A few cycles later, a new leader considered cancelling them. The team pushed back: "These sessions remind us why we changed." That's when the company realized the ritual had become cultural glue.

Sustainment means defending the quiet, unglamorous routines that make success reproducible.

Leader Moves:

- Keep the review rhythm alive, even when times get tough
- Rotate facilitators to refresh perspective
- Publicly acknowledge consistency, not just creativity, because endurance is built through reinforcement rather than reinvention.

4. Scale — Expand Only What's Stable

Most organizations scale prematurely, they replicate models before confirming that they work under pressure.

Scaling chaos only multiplies chaos.

Netflix's global expansion offers a masterclass in pacing. The company tested its "freedom and responsibility" culture in small markets before codifying it globally. Every principle was treated like a prototype, scaled only after it proved durable.

Change should behave like software releases: pilot → patch → upgrade → scale.

Leader Moves:

- Scale what's stable, not what's trendy
- Capture local learnings before replication
- Create a "scale score" — readiness based on consistency, not enthusiasm

The Loop in Motion

These four elements aren't linear. They're cyclical.

Chapter 13
Change That Sticks

When a company senses well, it simplifies early. When it simplifies, sustaining becomes easier. When it sustains, scaling becomes safer.

Leaders who master this loop treat transformation like a breathing organism, inhale learning, exhale focus.

A senior executive once told me, "Our culture used to feel like a race. Now it feels like a rhythm."

That's the essence of the sustainability loop, rhythm over rush, clarity over chaos, momentum over motion.

Because change doesn't stick through intensity. It sticks through intelligent repetition.

Leadership Moves and Reflection

Leaders don't make change last by designing better frameworks.

They make it last by embodying the message long after everyone else has moved on.

Organizations watch what leaders sustain more than what they start.

A launch meeting impresses people. A consistent example transforms them.

1. Be the Continuity in the Noise

Change always creates a spike of excitement followed by a valley of fatigue. That valley is where people look up to see if leadership still believes.

If you show up with the same clarity, patience, and conviction, especially when enthusiasm dips, the organization takes its cue from you.

Culture learns from persistence.

One leader I worked with had a simple rule: "I will not announce a new priority until the old one has become a reflex." It made her unpopular with those who wanted novelty, but beloved by those who wanted stability.

Consistency is the most underrated form of inspiration.

2. Use Symbolic Actions, Not Speeches

Words are powerful. Actions immortalize them.

When a CEO joined a team's Friday learning review unannounced, camera on, no slides, just listening, the message spread faster than any memo: learning mattered

Symbolic actions become folklore. They tell people what the organization respects.

As one employee told me later, "After that day, we stopped calling those sessions optional."

Transformation isn't sustained by policies. It's sustained by stories people choose to retell.

3. Keep Purpose Visible

The further you go into change, the more the why fades.

Repetition revives it.

Great leaders keep connecting daily tasks to the larger purpose. They remind teams not just what they're doing, but why it matters to customers, colleagues, and society.

When fatigue sets in, purpose is the fuel.

As the old saying goes: "People can endure almost any how if they have a why."

4. Celebrate the Maintainers

Every transformation celebrates pioneers — those who start.

Few celebrate maintainers — those who keep the flame alive.

Yet maintainers are the reason cultures endure. They are the quiet custodians of progress, the ones who keep rituals running and learning alive.

Acknowledge them publicly.

They turn intention into inheritance.

Reflection

Change is never a single leader's creation. It's a collective rehearsal for a better future.

But it endures only when leaders choose consistency over charisma, humility over headlines, and reinforcement over reinvention.

The true mark of leadership isn't how loudly change begins under you.

It's how quietly it continues after you're gone.

Because the final act of transformation is not victory; it is continuity.

Every organization dreams of transformation.

Few pause to ask the more important question: Can we sustain it?

Because change doesn't end when the project closes. It ends when the new way of working becomes the only way people remember.

In that moment, transformation turns from memory into muscle.

The Rhythm of Endurance

If trust is the operating system of leadership, then change is the periodic update.

And like every update, it fails not because it's unnecessary, but because it isn't installed fully.

Real transformation isn't about acceleration. It's about absorption.

It's not the speed of implementation that matters — it's the depth of internalization.

The best organizations I've seen don't treat change as a reaction to crisis. They treat it as a rhythm of renewal. They sense early, simplify constantly, sustain deliberately, and scale responsibly.

They understand that endurance isn't built by momentum. It's built by meaning.

The Cultural Shift

When leaders make change part of identity, they no longer need campaigns.

Employees don't wait for permission to innovate. They feel responsible for improvement. Every meeting, every reflection, every small experiment becomes a quiet act of maintenance.

That's what culture truly is: consistent behavior in the service of shared belief.

Change that sticks doesn't ask for celebration.

It simply shows up every day, unannounced but unmistakable, in how people decide, speak, and act.

The Final Thought

Change doesn't need new slogans. It needs steady hands.

When leadership moves from launching programs to nurturing patterns, the organization learns the deepest lesson of all: transformation isn't a phase. It's a way of living.

Because in the end, lasting change isn't about what we start.

It's about what we choose to keep doing once no one is watching.

Notice the people who quietly sustain progress when attention moves elsewhere. They are often the real leaders of the system.

Leadership endures not in initiatives, but in what keeps working when you step away.

A quiet companion to *Lead Less, Build More*

This mirror is not meant to create urgency. It is meant to create awareness.

You don't need to answer every question.
You don't need to act immediately.
Notice what lingers. That's where the work is.

How Leadership Shows Up (When You're Not Pushing)

- Where do I still confuse motion with impact?
- Where have I successfully stepped back and let the **system** carry responsibility?
- Where do people rely on me because the system is weak—and where does the system work without me?

Trust, Listening, and Influence

- Is trust strong enough here for people to disagree openly?
- Do I listen for what is unsaid, or only for what aligns?
- When progress happens, is it because of my authority, or because influence is distributed?

Clarity, Conflict, and Ownership

- Do I prioritize **clarity**, even when it creates discomfort?
- How do I respond when conflict appears—do I channel it or soften it?
- Do people around me **own outcomes**, or simply complete tasks?

Decisions and Direction

- Are decisions made as fast as their reversibility allows?
- Where do we take thoughtful, bold bets—and where do we default to safety?
- Do we treat technology (including AI) as a partner in judgment, or something to postpone?

Structure and Change

- Does our structure genuinely distribute authority, or just rearrange control?
- When change initiatives end, what actually continues?
- What behaviors persist without reminders, dashboards, or escalation?

If Progress Has Stalled, Pause Here

Before starting anything new, ask:

Which anchor failed?

- **Clarity** — Do people know what truly matters?
- **Capability** — Do they have the judgment to act?
- **Community** — Is trust strong enough to share ownership?
- **Cadence** — Is reinforcement built into everyday work?

Fix the weakest anchor first. Most transformations don't fail from lack of effort—they fail from neglecting one anchor.

A Final Reflection

Tell one story of continuity. Not what started—but what stayed.

Notice the people who quietly sustain progress when attention moves elsewhere.
They are often the real leaders of the system.

Leadership endures not in initiatives, but in what keeps working when you step away.

Epilogue

The Invitation of Kailash

Leadership Lessons from a Sacred Journey

After years of studying leadership in boardrooms, programs, and transformation rooms with too many slides and too little oxygen, I came to a simple realization:

The hardest change to sustain is the one within ourselves.

Structures evolve. Cultures adapt. Technology advances. But what truly endures is the inner rhythm of awareness—what guides a leader when the frameworks end and only judgment remains.

Sometime after writing the first draft of this book, I experienced a journey that brought this truth back—without a single PowerPoint in sight.

It wasn't a leadership retreat. It was a pilgrimage.

To a mountain that teaches through silence.

You Don't Do Kailash. You Are Allowed To.

Some journeys you plan. Others you are summoned to.

Mount Kailash belongs firmly in the second category. Unlike Everest or Kilimanjaro, nobody talks about conquering Kailash. The mountain is sacred to Hindus, Buddhists, Jains, and Bon. Pilgrims don't climb it; they circle it.

You don't "do" Kailash.

You are allowed to walk around it.

That single distinction changes everything.

It also quietly reveals something most leaders forget the moment they receive a title:

Leadership is permission, not possession.

Your people allow you to lead when they grant you trust.
Your organization allows you to lead when you add value.
The market allows you to lead when you remain relevant.

Like Kailash, leadership doesn't belong to you. You are allowed to hold it—temporarily, conditionally, humbly.

The Mountain's First Lesson: Authority Doesn't Announce Itself

The first time we saw Kailash from a distance, the bus fell silent. No one instructed us to be quiet; the mountain demanded it.

It rose stark from the plateau—its peak wrapped in a perpetual crown of snow—less like a climb and more like a throne.

I thought of boardrooms I'd sat in where leaders tried to manufacture authority with words, volume, and certainty.

Kailash offered a different kind of authority: silent, immovable, beyond explanation.

True authority doesn't need to announce itself.
It is recognized, not imposed.

The Altitude Lesson: Carry Less

The trek begins with optimism. Bags checked, jackets zipped, poles in hand. Everyone thinks they're prepared—because preparation looks easy at sea level.

Within a few kilometers, altitude negotiates with you. Your breath shortens. Your heart races. And suddenly, every extra kilo in your bag feels like a bad decision with interest added.

That's what execution does in organizations too. At the kickoff, everything looks neat: clean decks, tidy goals, high confidence. And then reality begins. Meetings multiply. Processes pile up. Vanity projects sneak in wearing the disguise of "strategic."

Altitude punishes extra weight. So do markets.

The smart trekker learns to carry less. The smart leader learns to simplify.

The Humbling: Humility Is Survival

By evening, our group had splintered into smaller clusters—some faster, some slower. A few looked visibly shaken. Oxygen dipped. Nausea surfaced. Doubts arrived without invitation.

For a moment, I caught myself thinking: Why didn't they prepare better? And almost immediately, I felt my own chest tighten.

Up here, nobody is immune.

The mountain doesn't grade you on résumé, income, or past performance. It levels everyone equally.

Humility isn't a posture at altitude.

It's survival.

In leadership, new terrain makes fools of overconfidence. The fact that you won in one context doesn't mean you can out-muscle the next. Humility isn't soft. It's strategic.

The Waiting Lesson: Waiting Is Work

On treks, you expect the challenge to come from walking. What surprised me at Kailash was how often the challenge came from not walking.

We waited at immigration counters. We waited when roads were blocked. We waited for weather to shift. We waited because someone needed rest.

Waiting wasn't an interruption.

It was part of the pilgrimage.

And that's when the lesson arrived:

Waiting is not wasted time. Waiting is work.

In corporate life, we treat waiting as failure—idle time, idle resources, "inefficiency." But Kailash reframed it for me. The Sherpas never fought the waiting. They folded it into the journey.

Leaders who can fold stillness into execution—rather than resenting it—build organizations that last.

The Golden Moment: Don't Confuse Motion with Meaning

After days of walking—dust, fatigue, monotony—we came around a bend.

Everyone was tired. Conversations had shrunk to silence. Then someone ahead gasped, and the line of trekkers stopped.

Epilogue

I looked up—and there it was.

The north face of Mount Kailash, rising sheer and magnificent, bathed in golden light. For a few minutes, it seemed to glow from within.

It wasn't scheduled. It wasn't in the itinerary. It certainly wasn't a KPI.

It was grace.

And it taught me something leadership metrics rarely capture:

Success is not always the summit. Sometimes it's the moment of alignment—when purpose, effort, and timing converge.

In companies, we measure outcomes. But the real golden moments are when the team feels the work matters—when alignment becomes palpable, when people glimpse something larger than themselves.

Your job as a leader is not to manufacture those moments.

Your job is to build the conditions where people are ready to receive them—and wise enough to recognize them.

Reflection: Lead Like a Guest of the Terrain

The trek ended, not with a triumphant "I conquered Kailash," but with a humbler truth:

I was allowed to.

The weather held. The Sherpas guided. My body cooperated. The mountain permitted.

Permission, not conquest.

And that phrase has become a leadership credo for me.

Leadership isn't Everest, where you plant a flag and declare victory.

Leadership is Kailash: a responsibility you are invited to hold for a time.

So before this book closes, I want to leave you with what the mountain left me—not as rules, not as hacks, but as invitations.

The Kailash Credo: Ten Invitations for Leaders

1. **Let authority be recognized, not announced.**
   If you need to keep reminding people you're in charge, you're not leading—you're compensating.
2. **Carry less.**
   Clutter kills momentum. Strip away what doesn't serve the mission.
3. **Treat humility as a strategy, not a virtue.**
   New terrain punishes overconfidence faster than your competitors ever will.
4. **Remember: leadership is permission, not possession.**
   Trust is not your entitlement. It's your lease—and it expires without renewal.
5. **Set thresholds and enforce them.**
   Collapse prevention is leadership. Red lines are not weakness; they are wisdom.
6. **Honor the house rules.**
   Constraints aren't insults. They're the terrain. Adapt inside them, not against them.
7. **Choose rituals over hype.**
   Transformation is carried by habits, not announcements. Discipline sustains what adrenaline starts.
8. **Manage energy before chasing distance.**
   The hidden economy is capacity. Teams don't fail only from lack of talent—they fail from exhaustion.

9. **Wait well.**
   Patience is not passive. It's active risk management. Stillness can be a strategic advantage.
10. **Lead with gratitude.**
    Gratitude is governance. It prevents fractures that policies can't repair.

Closing Thought

I didn't do Kailash. I was allowed to.

And leadership is no different.

You are allowed to lead—by your people, by your organization, by your context—for a season.

So lead like a guest of the terrain.

Carry the weight of responsibility lightly.
Walk with humility.
Honor the constraints.
Wait well.
And when those golden moments arrive, unscheduled flashes of meaning, recognize them.

Because in the end, leadership isn't about reaching the summit.

It's about how you walk—so others can walk farther after you.

The Thinking Behind the Book

This book brings together established research and lived leadership practice to explore how organizations scale without becoming dependent on individual heroes.

The ideas in *Lead Less, Build More* are informed by decades of work in organizational behavior, psychology, systems thinking, decision science, and management research. That research provides a foundation—but not a script. Throughout the book, evidence is used to inform judgment, not replace it.

Several research streams shape the arguments presented here:

Trust and Psychological Safety

Research by Amy Edmondson and large-scale studies such as Google's Project Aristotle show that trust and psychological safety enable learning, collaboration, and adaptability. This book builds on that work by examining how trust functions as an operating system—supporting performance when leaders intentionally step back and allow systems to carry responsibility.

Systems Thinking and Organizational Design

Insights from Donella Meadows, Peter Senge, and Henry Mintzberg inform the book's emphasis on leaders as designers of systems rather than sole decision-makers. The focus is on decision rights, feedback loops, and ownership structures that allow organizations to scale without increasing control.

Motivation, Autonomy, and Work Design

Self-Determination Theory (Deci & Ryan) and job design research (Hackman & Oldham) underpin the argument that autonomy alone is insufficient. Sustainable performance emerges when autonomy is paired with clarity of purpose, well-defined outcomes, and accountability.

Decision-Making and Judgment Under Uncertainty

Research by Daniel Kahneman, Philip Tetlock, and Max Bazerman shapes the discussion on bias, judgment, and decision velocity. Rather than promising perfect decisions, the book focuses on creating conditions where disagreement is surfaced early, learning is rapid, and decisions improve over time.

Productivity, Burnout, and Sustainable Performance

Findings from the OECD, economic research on working hours, and burnout studies by Maslach and Leiter inform the book's perspective on performance sustainability. The emphasis is not on effort as a signal of commitment, but on work design that supports endurance and consistent results.

Modern Scaling and Human–Technology Collaboration

Contemporary research on agile teams, distributed authority, and human–AI collaboration (including work by McChrystal, Brynjolfsson, Davenport, and McKinsey Global Institute) supports the book's focus on scaling judgment rather than dependency, while maintaining appropriate governance and accountability.

This book does not claim universal answers. Context matters, trade-offs are real, and leadership choices often involve tension rather than resolution. Research is treated as a lens, not a verdict—helping leaders decide when to intervene, when to step back, and when to redesign the system itself.

The bibliography that follows lists the primary works that informed this synthesis. The interpretations and applications reflect the author's experience leading large-scale transformations across geographies and cultures, where ideas are tested not in theory, but in execution.

Bibliography

Cirillo, F. (2006). *The Pomodoro Technique*.

Bazerman, M. H., & Moore, D. A. (2012). *Judgment in Managerial Decision Making* (8th ed.). Wiley.

Brynjolfsson, E., & McAfee, A. (2014). *The Second Machine Age: Work, Progress, and Prosperity in a Time of Brilliant Technologies*. W. W. Norton & Company.

Collins, J. (2001). *Good to Great: Why Some Companies Make the Leap... and Others Don't*. HarperBusiness.

Covey, S. M. R. (2006). *The Speed of Trust: The One Thing That Changes Everything*. Free Press.

Davenport, T. H., & Ronanki, R. (2018). Artificial intelligence for the real world. *Harvard Business Review*, 96(1), 108–116.

Deci, E. L., & Ryan, R. M. (2000). The "what" and "why" of goal pursuits: Human needs and the self-determination of behavior. *Psychological Inquiry*, 11(4), 227–268.

Dirks, K. T., & Ferrin, D. L. (2001). The role of trust in organizational settings. *Organization Science*, 12(4), 450–467.

Drucker, P. F. (2001). *The Essential Drucker*. HarperBusiness.

Edmondson, A. C. (2018). *The Fearless Organization: Creating Psychological Safety in the Workplace for Learning, Innovation, and Growth*. Wiley.

Edmondson, A. C. (2019). *The Right Kind of Wrong: The Science of Failing Well*. Atria Books.

Grant, A. (2021). *Think Again: The Power of Knowing What You Don't Know*. Viking.

"Performing a Project Premortem" — *Gary Klein, Harvard Business Review*, September 2007

Hackman, J. R. (2002). *Leading Teams: Setting the Stage for Great Performances*. Harvard Business School Press.

Hackman, J. R., & Oldham, G. R. (1976). Motivation through the design of work: Test of a theory. *Organizational Behavior and Human Performance*, 16(2), 250–279.

Hammond, J. S., Keeney, R. L., & Raiffa, H. (1999). *Smart Choices: A Practical Guide to Making Better Decisions*. Harvard Business School Press.

Heifetz, R., Grashow, A., & Linsky, M. (2009). *The Practice of Adaptive Leadership*. Harvard Business Press.

Kahneman, D. (2011). *Thinking, Fast and Slow*. Farrar, Straus and Giroux.

Kaplan, R. S., & Norton, D. P. (2001). *Strategy-Focused Organization*. Harvard Business School Press.

Laloux, F. (2014). *Reinventing Organizations: A Guide to Creating Organizations Inspired by the Next Stage of Human Consciousness*. Nelson Parker.

Maslach, C., & Leiter, M. P. (2016). Understanding the burnout experience. *World Psychiatry*, 15(2), 103–111.

McChrystal, S., Collins, T., Silverman, D., & Fussell, C. (2015). *Team of Teams: New Rules of Engagement for a Complex World*. Portfolio.

McKinsey Global Institute. (2023). *The State of AI in Organizations*. McKinsey & Company.

Meadows, D. H. (2008). *Thinking in Systems: A Primer*. Chelsea Green Publishing.

Mintzberg, H. (2009). *Managing*. Berrett-Koehler.

OECD. (2016). *Working Time and Productivity*. Organisation for Economic Co-operation and Development.

Pencavel, J. (2015). The productivity of working hours. *The Economic Journal*, 125(589), 2052–2076.

Pfeffer, J. (2010). *Power: Why Some People Have It—and Others Don't*. HarperBusiness.

Pink, D. H. (2009). *Drive: The Surprising Truth About What Motivates Us*. Riverhead Books.

Rumelt, R. P. (2011). *Good Strategy / Bad Strategy: The Difference and Why It Matters*. Crown Business.

Senge, P. M. (1990). *The Fifth Discipline: The Art and Practice of the Learning Organization*. Doubleday.

Sinek, S. (2014). *Leaders Eat Last*. Portfolio.

Tetlock, P. E., & Gardner, D. (2015). *Superforecasting: The Art and Science of Prediction*. Crown.

Weick, K. E. (1995). *Sensemaking in Organizations*. Sage Publications.

Google re:Work. (2016). *Project Aristotle: Understanding Team Effectiveness*. Google Inc.

www.ingramcontent.com/pod-product-compliance
Lightning Source LLC
Chambersburg PA
CBHW031609210526
45464CB00004B/1488